P · O · C · K · E · T · S

FOSSILS

TYLOCIDARIS
(SEA URCHIN)

BOSTRYCHOCERAS
(AMMONITE)

BIRKENIA
(FISH)

P · O · C · K · E · T · S

FOSSILS

Written by
DOUGLAS PALMER

STAURANDERASTER
(STARFISH)

DIPLOCAULUS
(AMPHIBIAN)

CENOCERAS
(NAUTILOID)

A DK PUBLISHING BOOK

Project editor Clint Twist
Art editor Sarah Crouch
Senior editor Hazel Egerton
Senior art editor Jacquie Gulliver
Picture research Jo Walton
Production Josie Alabaster
US editor Jill Hamilton

First American Edition 1996
2 4 6 8 10 9 7 5 3 1
Published in the United States by DK Publishing, Inc.,
95 Madison Avenue, New York, New York 10016

Library of Congress Cataloging-in-Publication Data

Palmer, Douglas
  Fossils / by Douglas Palmer.- - 1st American ed.
    p. cm. - - (Pockets)
  Includes index
  Summary: Introduces the world of fossils including information on where
  they are found, how they are formed, and how they are classified; also
  describes many of the various kinds.
  ISBN 0-7894-0606-3
  1. Fossils - - Juvenile literature. [1. Fossils.] I. Title. II. Series
QE714.5p26 1996
560--dc20   95-42178
                                                                 CIP
                                                                  AC

Color reproduction by Colourscan, Singapore
Printed and bound in Italy by L.E.G.O.

CONTENTS

HOW TO USE THIS BOOK

These pages show you how to use *Pockets: Fossils*. The book is divided into five sections. Each section contains information on different aspects of fossils or fossil collecting. At the beginning of each section there is a picture page and a guide to the contents of that section.

HEADING
This describes the subject of the page. This page is about gastropods. If a subject continues over several pages, the same heading applies.

INTRODUCTION
This provides you with a summary and overview of the subject. After reading the introduction, you should have a clear idea of what the following page, or pages, are about.

CORNER CODING
The corners of the main section pages are color coded to remind you which section you are in.

■ INVERTEBRATES
■ VERTEBRATES
■ PLANTS

GEOLOGIC PERIODS
In this book, fossils are dated according to their geologic periods. In many cases, a more precise dating is indicated by the use of *Early (E.)*, *Middle (M.)*, and *Late (L.)*.

Corner coding

INVERTEBRATES

GASTROPODS
FAMILIAR TODAY as garden slugs and snails, gastropods inhabit a wide variety of habitats: marine, freshwater, and terrestrial. Most gastropods are plant-eaters, and their fossils are frequently found in shallow-water deposits, where aquatic plants would have been most plentiful.

Heading

Introduction

Annotation

AUSTRALIS
L. Cretaceous–Recent
Most gastropod shells coil to the right (dextrally). *Australis*, however, has a shell that coils to the left (sinistrally). The shell is thin, like that of most freshwater gastropods.

Caption

Fact box

GASTROPOD FACTS
• More than 15,000 fossil species of gastropod have so far been discovered.
• Most gastropods are plant-eaters, but some marine species hunt other mollusks, and even small fish.

Bivalve
inner coils

PLATE SHAIL
Silurian–Mississippian
Fossils of this gastropod are sometimes found attached to coral cups. *Platyceras* shells are draped to fit around the cups, and it is believed that the gastropod obtained its food from corals.

Geologic periods
FACT BOXES
Many pages have fact boxes. These provide at-a-glance information about the subject, such as the number of fossil species that have been discovered.

8

RUNNING HEADS
These remind you which section you are in. The top of the left-hand page gives the section name, and the top of the right-hand page gives the subject heading.

LABELS
For extra clarity, some pictures have labels. These identify a picture if it is not immediately obvious what it is from the text, or they may give extra information.

LIFE ILLUSTRATION
Many of the fossils in this book have an illustration to show what the organism looked like when alive.

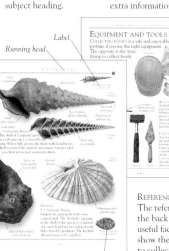

Label

Running head

REFERENCE SECTION
The reference pages are yellow and appear at the back of the book. On these, you will find useful facts, figures, and charts. These pages show the equipment and tools you need in order to collect fossils safely.

Life illustration

CAPTIONS AND ANNOTATIONS
Each illustration is accompanied by a caption. Annotations, in *italics*, point out the features of an illustration, and usually have leader lines.

INDEX AND GLOSSARY
At the back of the book is an index listing every subject in the book. By referring to the index, information on particular topics can be found quickly. A glossary defines the technical terms used in the book.

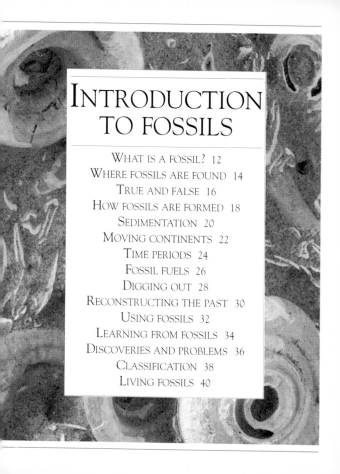

INTRODUCTION
TO FOSSILS

WHAT IS A FOSSIL?

A FOSSIL IS the preserved evidence of a once-living plant or animal. The word fossil means "dug out of the ground," and most fossils are found preserved in layers of rock. The most common fossils are skeletal remains such as shells, teeth, and bones. Fossils that preserve soft tissues are very rare.

LARGE TOOTH
FROM UPPER JAW

*Sharp-edged
tooth of a
meat-eater*

Tooth root

SMALL TOOTH
FROM LOWER JAW

SHARK'S TEETH
There is no mistaking these daggerlike fossil teeth. They look like the teeth of a living shark, but are millions of years old. Teeth are made of calcium phosphate minerals that preserve very well.

FOSSIL FACTS
• The most common fossils are the shells of marine animals.
• The first marine animals with shells appeared in the fossil record about 570 million years ago.

*Plaster has been
colored to match
the original*

GALLIMIMUS
The scientific study of important fossils often requires that accurate copies are made. This is a plaster cast of the skull of an ostrichlike dinosaur. It was cast from a mold taken from the original skull.

CRUZIANA
Fossils that preserve the tracks or burrows made by animals in the past are called trace fossils. *Cruziana* is the scientific name given to the tracks in sea-bottom mud that are believed to have been made by trilobites as they fed.

Trilobite feeding burrows

Hardened sediment preserves what was once a sea floor

PRESERVED IN ROCK
This split rock reveals the upper surface of an extinct trilobite. The animal's remains were dissolved but its shape was preserved as a natural mold and cast.

INSECT IN AMBER
Amber is fossilized tree resin which sometimes preserves trapped insects. This wasp is more than 100 million years old, but every detail is preserved. DNA has been successfully extracted from insects trapped in amber.

WHERE FOSSILS ARE FOUND

MOST FOSSILS ARE FOUND in sedimentary rocks that are exposed at the surface. Rocks that contain many fossils are called fossiliferous. The most common fossiliferous rocks are limestones, sandstones, and shales. The types of fossils contained in the rock depend on the type of environment in which the sediment was originally laid down. Marine sediments, from coastlines and shallow seas, usually contain the most fossils.

MASSIVE TRACE FOSSILS
The lower surfaces of these sandstone rocks preserve an ancient sea floor. Earth movements have uplifted and tilted the rocks, while coastal erosion has exposed the trace fossils.

DESERT ROCKS
Fossil-bearing sedimentary rocks are often well exposed in deserts that are associated with mountain belts. In the Andean foothills of Chile, a single 6-ft (2-m) thick layer of rock contains thousands of fossilized bones like the one shown above.

CAVE DEPOSITS
Caves, which provide shelter for animals, are a good source of recent fossils. This cave in Utah contains a 16-in (40-cm) layer of fossilized mammoth dung. Analysis of the plant remains in the dung has given valuable information about the diet of the extinct mammoth.

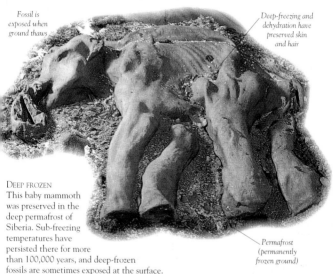

Fossil is exposed when ground thaws

Deep-freezing and dehydration have preserved skin and hair

DEEP FROZEN
This baby mammoth was preserved in the deep permafrost of Siberia. Sub-freezing temperatures have persisted there for more than 100,000 years, and deep-frozen fossils are sometimes exposed at the surface.

Permafrost (permanently frozen ground)

TRUE AND FALSE

IN THE EARLY DAYS of science, anything that was dug out of the ground was called a fossil. Some of these were true fossils – the remains of once-living organisms. Others were false fossils – objects that just happened to resemble organic remains. A few were deliberate forgeries designed to deceive unwary collectors into parting with money for "rare" fossils.

FLINT LEG
This is not a fossil, but a Cretaceous flint more than 65 million years old. Flints are made of silica, often from dissolved sponge spicules, and do not have a crystal structure. Within some sedimentary rocks such as chalk, they can grow into almost any shape.

Weathered outer surface of flint

MOSSY MINERALS
These mosslike growths in rock are actually mineral deposits. Manganese and a number of other minerals form branching crystals that are often mistaken for fossil plants.

CHIASTOLITE

These are not fossils, but rod-shaped crystals of an aluminum silicate mineral called chiastolite. The crystals were formed in the surrounding rock matrix as a result of intense heating within the Earth's crust.

Crystals of chiastolite

Rock matrix

GRAPTOLITES

These are real fossils. They are a type of graptolite whose small, branching fossil colonies look like tuning forks. The organic skeleton of this colony has been altered into a white claylike mineral during fossilization.

Hand-carved snake's head

SNAKE STONE

This is both a true and false fossil. Someone has carved a snake's head at the broken end of a fossil Jurassic ammonite. This sort of embellishment was quite common in the past, and was not always designed to deceive. Some altered fossils were intended as good-luck charms to ward off evil spirits, while others were purely decorative.

HOW FOSSILS ARE FORMED

FOSSILS ARE FORMED by the processes of decay at
work in the remains of once living organisms. This
often occurs when plant or animal remains become
buried in an oxygen-free environment. The remains
are rarely preserved in their original form. In many
cases, their mineral content is altered
chemically, or the remains dissolved
completely to be replaced by
a cast.

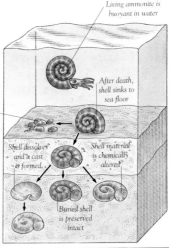

*Living ammonite is
buoyant in water*

AMMONITE FOSSIL
This fossil is a natural cast.
The shell has dissolved,
leaving a mold, which
has filled with sediment.

*Shell breaks
up and may
not be
preserved*

*After death,
shell sinks to
sea floor*

FOSSILIZATION AT SEA
Dead plants and animals sink to the
sea floor, where their bodies either
decay or become buried in sediment.
As the sediment gradually hardens
into rock, body parts may be
chemically altered, or even dissolved
to leave a cavity. This cavity may
then become filled with minerals that
harden to form a natural cast.

*Shell dissolves
and a cast
is formed*

*Shell material
is chemically
altered*

*Buried shell
is preserved
intact*

FOSSILIZATION ON LAND

1. An animal body lies decaying on the surface of the land. .

2. Wind or water deposit sand and mud, covering the body.

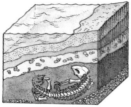

3. Over time, the bones are altered, and the sand and mud turn to rock.

4. Weathering and erosion expose the fossil at the surface.

ASPHALT LAKE

Land animals are only fossilized under exceptional conditions. Normally their remains are scattered and decay. At the La Brea tar pits in California, thousands of fossils have been found in a natural asphalt lake. The animals were attracted by water on the asphalt surface and became trapped.

SEDIMENTATION

WEATHERING AND EROSION on land and at sea produce large quantities of sediment, which is usually laid down in strata (layers). The size and shape of sedimentary deposits depend on the process by which the sediments were laid down. Beach and river sands produce ribbon-shaped deposits. Mud particles in lakes and oceans are deposited in thin sheets. Over millions of years, these deposits harden into rock.

DESERT CLIFFS
These cliffs show sandstone strata. The oldest deposits are the lowest strata, with the most recent deposits at the top. The color of these rocks and the way they are cross-bedded (with layers arranged at different angles) are typical of wind-blown desert deposits.

SEDIMENTATION FACT
• If there were a place where sediments had been deposited continuously since Cambrian times, the resulting sedimentary rock strata would now be more than 100 miles (160 km) deep.

Lime-rich sediment collects on sea floor   *Limestone*

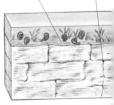

BENEATH THE SEA
Seabed deposits vary according to depth and energy conditions. Quiet, deep waters have fine-grained mud. Shallow waters tend to have coarse-grained particles.

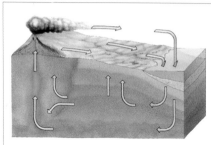

ROCK CYCLE
Landscapes are
continuously reduced
by the processes of
erosion. Particle by
particle, mountains are
carried to the sea to
become sediment.
The cycle is completed
where volcanoes and
earth movements bring
new rock to the surface.

DESERTS AND DELTAS
Desert sanddunes produce distinctive
sandstones with rounded grains.
River deltas produce vast quantities
of sand and mud. The weight of the
newer deposits compresses the older
deposits underneath.

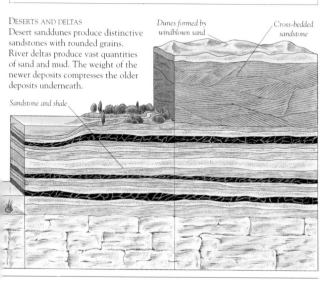

Dunes formed by windblown sand

Cross-bedded sandstone

Sandstone and shale

MOVING CONTINENTS

ONE OF THE GREATEST discoveries of modern science
is the fact that the continents are in constant slow-
motion. Over geological time, rising heat from Earth's
interior creates new ocean floor and moves continents
apart. Sometimes the continents collide to form
supercontinents, such as Pangaea. These collisions
can also create mountain ranges.

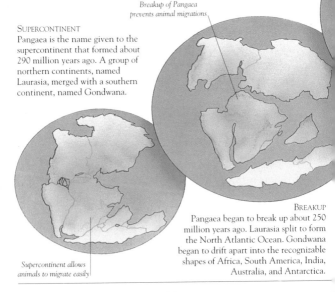

*Breakup of Pangaea
prevents animal migrations*

SUPERCONTINENT
Pangaea is the name given to the
supercontinent that formed about
290 million years ago. A group of
northern continents, named
Laurasia, merged with a southern
continent, named Gondwana.

*Supercontinent allows
animals to migrate easily*

BREAKUP
Pangaea began to break up about 250
million years ago. Laurasia split to form
the North Atlantic Ocean. Gondwana
began to drift apart into the recognizable
shapes of Africa, South America, India,
Australia, and Antarctica.

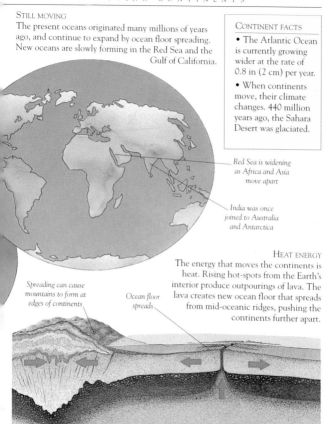

STILL MOVING
The present oceans originated many millions of years ago, and continue to expand by ocean floor spreading. New oceans are slowly forming in the Red Sea and the Gulf of California.

CONTINENT FACTS
• The Atlantic Ocean is currently growing wider at the rate of 0.8 in (2 cm) per year.

• When continents move, their climate changes. 440 million years ago, the Sahara Desert was glaciated.

Red Sea is widening as Africa and Asia move apart

India was once joined to Australia and Antarctica

HEAT ENERGY
The energy that moves the continents is heat. Rising hot-spots from the Earth's interior produce outpourings of lava. The lava creates new ocean floor that spreads from mid-oceanic ridges, pushing the continents further apart.

Spreading can cause mountains to form at edges of continents

Ocean floor spreads

TIME PERIODS

GEOLOGICAL TIME PERIODS are based on the sequence of rock strata (layers), with the oldest strata at the bottom. The sequence was worked out by matching

sedimentary rocks and their fossils around the world. The main subdivisions of this sequence represent major changes in the global environment. The age in years is estimated using chemical information from granite rock.

BREAK IN STRATA
Here, there is a major gap in sedimentation. Present-day soil lies on top of old, tilted, and eroded strata.

TIME PERIOD FACTS

• Some geological periods are named after areas where rocks from that period are well exposed, e.g., the Jura mountains of France.

• The Carboniferous period is so named because large amounts of carbon (in the form of coal) were laid down during that period.

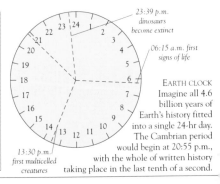

23:39 p.m. dinosaurs become extinct

06:15 a.m. first signs of life

13:30 p.m. first multicelled creatures

EARTH CLOCK
Imagine all 4.6 billion years of Earth's history fitted into a single 24-hr day. The Cambrian period would begin at 20:55 p.m., with the whole of written history taking place in the last tenth of a second.

PERIOD	EPOCH
QUATERNARY	HOLOCENE
	PLEISTOCENE
TERTIARY	PLIOCENE
	MIOCENE
	OLIGOCENE
	EOCENE
	PALEOCENE

MYA	PERIOD		ERA
2	QUATERNARY		CENOZOIC
65	TERTIARY		
144	CRETACEOUS		MESOZOIC
208	JURASSIC		
248	TRIASSIC		
286	PERMIAN		PALEOZOIC
320	CARBONIFEROUS	PENNSYLVANIAN (North America)	
360		MISSISSIPPIAN (North America)	
408	DEVONIAN		
438	SILURIAN		
505	ORDOVICIAN		
550	CAMBRIAN		
	PRECAMBRIAN TIME		

NAMING THE PAST
Geologists have identified and named the intervals of geological time. The largest units are eras. These are divided into periods, which are subdivided into epochs. Fossils are used to divide epochs into smaller units.

FOSSIL FUELS

COAL, OIL, AND NATURAL GAS are fossil fuels derived from the decay of plant and animal tissue. Most organic remains decay into gases that are lost to the atmosphere, but at times of high productivity, some remains get trapped in sediment. Marine microorganisms decay to form oil and natural gas. Land plants decay to form peat, coal, and gas.

CRUDE OIL

1. Marine organisms die and are buried beneath the seabed

2. Oil and natural gas form in porous sedimentary rock

SEA FLOOR FUELS
Vast quantities of organic material have accumulated over time in seabed sediments. As the organic material has decayed, it has released enormous quantities of oil and gas.

3. Oil and gas move upward

4. Oil and gas trapped by nonporous rock

OIL AND GAS FORMATION

COAL
FORMATION

Forests grow well in hot, swampy conditions

PEAT

The trees eventually die, and are covered with swamp sediment

BITUMINOUS COAL

Plant remains compressed into a layer of peat

Peat is compressed into lignite

COAL

From Pennsylvanian and Mississippian times, there has been an extensive growth of vegetation in the humid Tropics. Plant debris was trapped between layers of sediment. Over time, increasing pressure has compressed the debris, first into peat, then lignite (brown coal), and then bituminous coal.

Coal seam (layer of coal)

DIGGING OUT

BEING A FOSSIL HUNTER is like being a detective. The rock surrounding the fossil may contain clues as to how the organism lived and died. It must be carefully examined and samples taken. Only when this evidence has been gathered should the fossil be removed. Although fossils are often heavy, they are also fragile. Considerable care and attention to safety is required.

WIDESPREAD EXCAVATION
At this site, some dinosaur footprints have been unearthed. A wide area is being excavated to reveal any further tracks.

INTENSIVE SEARCH
Success in finding fossils is often the result of long hours of hard work. These Chinese fossil hunters are carefully splitting pieces of 530-million-year-old rock. Each piece of rock must be examined with an expert eye in case it contains a rare fossil.

HAPPY HUNTERS
Two volunteer fossil hunters proudly display the rewards of their hard work – the bone of an extinct mammoth. By sifting through many tons (tonnes) of mud and sand, they were eventually able to find almost the entire skeleton.

Soft brush removes mud

Freshly excavated fossil

FOSSIL WASHING
When first excavated, most fossils still have some sediment attached to them. Soft mud and sand can be washed off with water. Tougher sediment and fragments of rock matrix must be removed later with a variety of special tools.

RECONSTRUCTING THE PAST

FLESHING OUT a fossil skeleton helps us see fossils as once-living creatures, and tests our ideas about their biology. This can be difficult with extinct animals that have no close living relatives. The posture of some dinosaurs has been reinterpreted several times.

TRICERATOPS – THE BARE BONES
Assembling a fossil skeleton is difficult. With the extinct dinosaurs, there is the added problem of posture. The limbs of living reptiles stick out sideways, but in this posture they could not support *Triceratops'* large body. So instead, the dinosaur has been given a mammal-like posture.

Limbs placed in a mammal-like posture beneath the body, rather than sticking out sideways like surviving reptiles

Metal frame to support skeleton

RECONSTRUCTING FROM A SKELETON

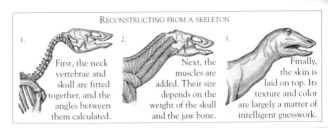

1. First, the neck vertebrae and skull are fitted together, and the angles between them calculated.

2. Next, the muscles are added. Their size depends on the weight of the skull and the jaw bone.

3. Finally, the skin is laid on top. Its texture and color are largely a matter of intelligent guesswork.

LIFELIKE MODEL

Striped "camouflage" coloring would have helped conceal Triceratops from hungry predators

TRICERATOPS – RECONSTRUCTION
Here, the complete skeleton has been "clothed" in skin and muscle. Fossil bones often bear scars where the muscles were attached in life. These scars enable scientists to position muscles accurately when reconstructing an extinct body form. Fossils very rarely give any clues to an animal's coloring. The colors seen here are based on the sorts of color-schemes found on living reptiles.

RECONSTRUCTED SKELETON

Mammoth model on display in museum

MAMMOTH DISPLAY
Extinct mammoths are easily modeled using information obtained from the study of modern elephants. This model has been placed in an accurate reconstruction of an ice age environment.

USING FOSSILS

FOSSILS ARE VITAL to understanding the history of Earth's sedimentary rocks. The subdivision of geological time and the matching of rock strata both depend on fossils. Organisms change over time, and these changes are used to mark time periods. For example, any rocks containing graptolite fossils must date from the Paleozoic era. The geographical distribution of fossils enables geologists to match rock strata from many different parts of the world.

EXPANSOGRAPTUS
This fossil graptolite has a worldwide geographical distribution, but a fairly narrow distribution in time. Any rocks containing this fossil are Ordovician.

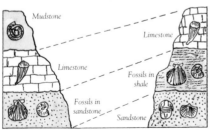

MATCHING STRATA
Many organisms were restricted to a particular habitat, and their fossils to one type of rock. Most fossil corals can be matched only between limestones. Others, such as ammonites and bivalves, occur in a wider range and enable scientists to match sandstone and shale strata.

Mudstone

Limestone

Limestone

Fossils in shale

Fossils in sandstone

Sandstone

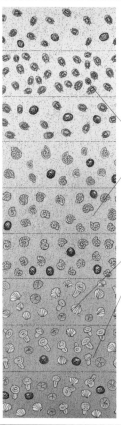

DEFINING FOSSIL ZONES

Some fossils, called index fossils, can be used to divide rock strata into zones. The zone where the index fossil is most abundant is called the acme zone of that fossil. A zone where two or more index fossils are present is called the concurrent range zone of those fossils.

Acme zone
of trilobites

Concurrent
range zone
of different
ammonite
species

Acme zone
of bivalves

Acme zone
of corals

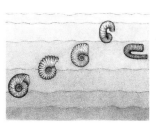

FOSSIL DATING

Fossils change over time as generation succeeds generation. These strata have been subdivided according to the changes in the shape of ammonites they contain.

KEY

 TRILOBITES

 AMMONITES

 BIVALVES

 CORALS

 SEA URCHINS

FOSSIL FACTS

• The time periods defined by index fossils can be as short as two million years.

• Abrupt changes in the sequence of fossils may indicate some form of natural catastrophe.

LEARNING FROM FOSSILS

FOSSILS OFTEN PRESERVE extinct organisms. Only by interpreting the preserved remains can we see them as once-living plants and animals. Our interpretation of fossils is based on our understanding of living organisms and present-day environments. But one of the most important lessons to be learned from fossils is that the history of life has taken place against an ever-changing background.

Leaves fossilized as dry films of carbon

Leaves shaped like those of modern banana plant

Shale formed from freshwater mud

FOSSIL FACTS

• Sites with especially good preservation, such as the Burgess Shale, show us just how much information is lost during the "normal" process of fossilization.

• Fossil coral has been found on Mt. Everest.

GLOSSOPTERIS
This fossil plant, which grew in a warm, wet climate, has been found in rocks of Permian age in India, South Africa, Australia, South America, and Antarctica. The fossils show that these places were once joined together and enjoyed the same subtropical climate.

TYPICAL HEIGHT
26 FT (8 M)

LIVING WINGS

Living dragonflies have two pairs of outstretched wings. The pattern of veins in the wings differs from species to species. Here, the wings are camouflaged to provide concealment from predators. Such fine details as these are only very rarely preserved in fossils.

Vein pattern can be compared with modern species

FOSSIL WING

This rare fossil has preserved the structure of a dragonfly wing as it was in life. The pattern of veins can be compared with living dragonflies to establish its species. The camouflage on the wing has also been preserved.

Protocardia shell

Myophorella shell

SHELLFISH COMMUNITY

This sandstone is packed with fossil bivalves of more than one species. By studying such natural assemblages, scientists can estimate the relative size of the populations of the various shellfish species in an ancient seabed community.

DISCOVERIES AND PROBLEMS

THE FOSSIL RECORD has so far only revealed a tiny fraction of the diversity of life that has existed on Earth. Only a few hundred thousand fossil species have been described, and millions more await discovery. For the fossil hunter, the chances of finding a new species are quite high. However, the quality of preservation varies enormously, and accurate identification of a fossil species may be very difficult.

Hairs are fringed with tiny filaments

Matrix has been dissolved by acids

FILTER HAIRS
This perfectly preserved fossil is less than 0.008 in (0.2 mm) across, and more than 500 million years old. These delicate filter hairs were part of the feeding apparatus of an extinct crustacean.

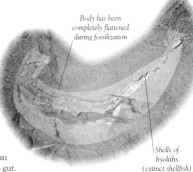

Body has been completely flattened during fossilization

OTTOIA
The soft body of this segmented worm from the Burgess Shale has been preserved in remarkable detail. The fossil provides a rare insight into the lifestyle of the animal. The remains of its last meal (hyolith shells) can be seen within its gut.

Shells of hyoliths (extinct shellfish)

PROBLEMATICA

This Ediacaran fossil has been identified as a jellyfish-type animal. However, the nature of its preservation as a sandstone cast suggests that its body tissues were quite different from any known jellyfish.

Central, button-like protuberance

Concentric lobes

PERCENTAGE PRESERVATION

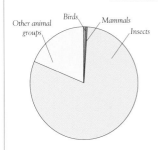

Other animal groups
Birds
Mammals
Insects

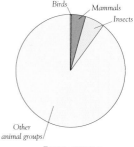

Birds
Mammals
Insects
Other animal groups

LIVING ANIMALS

Of the 1,000,000 or so living animal species that have been named, about 80% are insects. Of the remaining species, 0.45% are mammals and 0.9% are birds. All other animal groups make up only 18.65%.

FOSSIL ANIMALS

Of the approximately 200,000 fossil animal species that have been discovered, only about 6% are insects. 4% are mammals and 0.5% are birds. Other animal groups, mainly shellfish, make up the remaining 89.5%.

CLASSIFICATION

TO DESCRIBE the variety of life, organisms must be separated into biologically meaningful groups. The basic unit of classification is the species, which is given a unique two-part name in Latin. Species may be classified in groups according to shared characteristics. The larger the group, the fewer the shared characteristics.

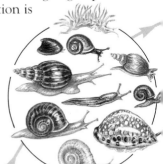

CLASS GASTROPODA

PHYLUM MOLLUSCA

PHYLUM MOLLUSCA
This large group contains animals with a wide variety of shapes from bivalves to octopuses. However, they all share internal features that identify them as mollusks. Important fossil mollusks are bivalves, gastropods, nautiloids, ammonoids, and belemnites.

CLASS GASTROPODA
The snails, slugs, and sea-hares have similar biological characteristics. Of the gastropods, only the shelled snails have a fossil history; the others leave no fossil evidence.

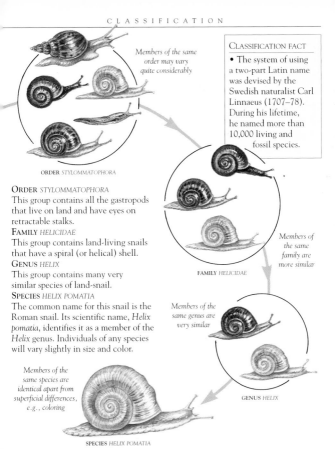

Members of the same order may vary quite considerably

CLASSIFICATION FACT

• The system of using a two-part Latin name was devised by the Swedish naturalist Carl Linnaeus (1707–78). During his lifetime, he named more than 10,000 living and fossil species.

ORDER *STYLOMMATOPHORA*

ORDER *STYLOMMATOPHORA*
This group contains all the gastropods that live on land and have eyes on retractable stalks.

FAMILY *HELICIDAE*
This group contains land-living snails that have a spiral (or helical) shell.

GENUS *HELIX*
This group contains many very similar species of land-snail.

SPECIES *HELIX POMATIA*
The common name for this snail is the Roman snail. Its scientific name, *Helix pomatia*, identifies it as a member of the *Helix* genus. Individuals of any species will vary slightly in size and color.

FAMILY *HELICIDAE*

Members of the same family are more similar

Members of the same genus are very similar

Members of the same species are identical apart from superficial differences, e.g., coloring

GENUS *HELIX*

SPECIES *HELIX POMATIA*

LIVING FOSSILS

THE TERM "LIVING FOSSIL" was first used by Charles Darwin to describe the ginkgo tree. The term refers to a living species that has survived over long periods of geologic time to the present day. The reason for these survivals is still unclear. The most likely explanation is that "living fossils" have adapted to habitats that have been continuously available over long periods.

MODERN
HORSESHOE CRAB

Telson
(tail spike)

HORSESHOE CRAB
These misnamed animals are not crabs but limulids – the only survivors of a once large group of arthropods. Their shape and lifestyle have changed very little during the past 400 million years.

LIVING FOSSIL FACTS

• The tuatara is the sole survivor of a reptile group that lived alongside dinosaurs.

• The mollusks have more living fossils than any other animal group.

MESOLIMULUS
(L. JURASSIC)

FOSSIL
LINGULA
(*PERMIAN*)

LINGULA   *Pedicle*
This brachiopod and its close relatives
have the longest fossil history of any
animal group. They have survived by
burrowing into the muddy sand on the
bottom of shallow seas for more than
430 million years.

COELACANTH
This is the most famous living
fossil, and the sole survivor of the
lobe-finned fishes. It was thought
to have died out 65 million years
ago. However, in 1947 a live
specimen was caught off the coast
of southern Africa.

FOSSIL COELACANTH
(*L. JURASSIC*)

*Bony, lobe-shaped
pectoral fin*

41

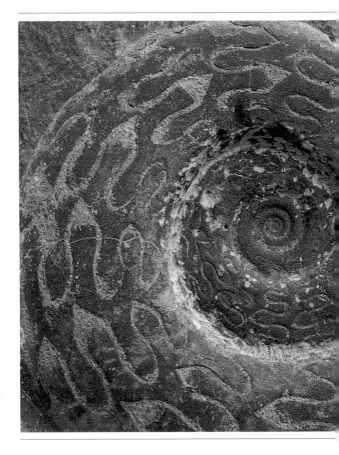

INVERTEBRATES

EARLIEST FOSSILS

THE FOSSIL EVIDENCE for life on Earth extends back some 3.5 billion years. The oldest fossils consist of single-celled plants and animals. The earliest evidence of multicelled life, such as worms and sea pens, comes from Ediacaran-type fossils, named after the region in Australia where they were discovered. These fossils date from about 700 million years ago.

Red coloration caused by oxidation of iron

IRONSTONE
The bands in this ironstone provide fossil evidence of seasonal variation in the amount of oxygen produced by microorganisms about 2 billion years ago.

FOSSIL FACTS

• The oldest fossil algae were found in Canada and are between 700–1,000 million years old.

• Ediacaran-type fossils have now been found at more than 20 different locations throughout the world.

Each cryptarch measures about 0.01 in (0.25 mm) across

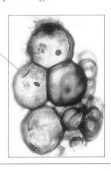

MICROFOSSILS
These primitive cell-like fossils are called cryptarchs. They have been chemically dissolved out of rock that is more than 1.4 billion years old. Like some modern cells, cryptarchs have a toughened organic wall.

STROMATOLITES

Stromatolites like these
have been produced by
microorganisms in shallow
seas for the past 3.5 billion
years. Colonies of algae
trap layers of sediment
that gradually build up
into mounds.
Stromatolites from
Australia are among the
oldest known fossils.

CHARNIA

This feather-shaped fossil is believed
to be a natural cast of a fossil sea
pen (a soft-bodied animal).
Charnia is one of the most
widespread of the Ediacaran-
type fossils. This specimen,
which was found in Britain,
is 640 million years old.

*Fine-grained
sandstone*

SPRIGGINA

The characteristics of this Ediacaran fossil
suggest that it was an early type of
annelid worm. The body has
about 40 segments and the
head is crescent-shaped
with long, hairlike
spines. Some scientists
believe that *Spriggina*
was an ancestor
of the trilobites.

*Crescent-shaped
head*

TYPICAL LENGTH
2.75 IN (7 CM)

SPONGES

FOR 600 MILLION YEARS sponges have lived
attached to the floor of the world's oceans.
These simple animals have a porous
body wall, often reinforced by a
skeleton of tiny mineral spicules
(spines). This skeleton may be
preserved as a fossil.
Sponges are classified
according to the mineral
content of their spicules.

SPONGE BEADS
Porosphaera, a
small Cretaceous
sponge, has a
spherical skeleton
with a central opening.
Bronze Age people used
the opening to string
these common fossils
into a necklace.

SKELETON CUP
The irregular and
fused spicules of this
calcareous sponge have
preserved its original
cup shape for more than
65 million years. Calcareous
sponges have spicules of
calcium carbonate.

Outer wall

Inner wall

Central
cavity

METALDETES
Cambrian
This fossil belongs to an extinct group
of small spongelike
animals called
archaeocyathids. This
cross-section through
the body shows that
the animal's skeleton
has been preserved in
great detail.

TYPICAL HEIGHT
2 IN (5 CM)

TYPICAL HEIGHT
4 IN (10 CM)

Slotlike pores trapped food

RHIZOPOTERION
Cretaceous
Glass sponges have spicules of silica. In this species, the spicules were fused to provide additional reinforcement for the thin walls with their slotlike pores. Seawater was sieved through these pores to remove food particles. In life, the sponge body was held upright on the seabed by root structures. These are broken off in most fossil specimens.

Open meshwork of sponge skeleton

HYDNOCERAS
L. Devonian–Pennsylvanian
An internal sandstone mold closely replicates the knobbly, vase shape of this glass sponge. The meshwork of silica spicules has impressed its rectangular pattern onto the surface of the mold.

Bulbous swelling

Rectangular meshwork

TYPICAL HEIGHT
8 IN (20 CM)

CORALS

LIVING CORAL ANIMALS are small polyps, like upside-down jellyfish. They produce a calcareous cup, called a corallite, in which they live. All that remains in fossil corals are individual corallites, or colonies of them. There have been three main types of coral. Rugose and tabulate corals are now extinct. Scleractinian corals are known from both living and fossil species.

Vertical septa

GALAXEA
This fossil specimen shows the typical features of a colonial coral, with individual corallites growing closely together.

Corallites

HALYSITES
M. Ordovician–L. Silurian
This tabulate coral is known as chain coral because the polyps bud to form chains. Corallites link together to create distinctive fencelike colonies.

Sediment between chains

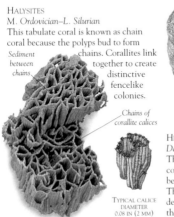

Chains of corallite calices

TYPICAL CALICE DIAMETER
0.08 IN (2 MM)

Calice with vertical septa

TYPICAL CALICE DIAMETER
0.75 IN (2 CM)

Growth ridges

HELIOPHYLLUM
Devonian
This type of tabulate coral is known as horn coral because of the shape of the corallite. The polyp lived in a shallow, cup-shaped depression (calice), divided internally by thin vertical plates known as septa.

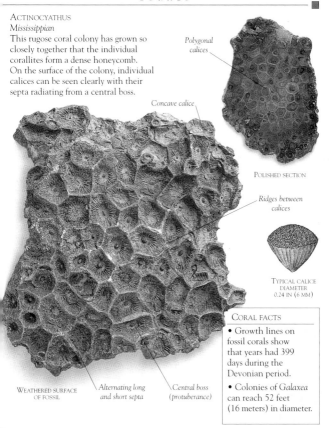

ACTINOCYATHUS
Mississippian
This rugose coral colony has grown so
closely together that the individual
corallites form a dense honeycomb.
On the surface of the colony, individual
calices can be seen clearly with their
septa radiating from a central boss.

Polygonal calices

Concave calice

POLISHED SECTION

Ridges between calices

TYPICAL CALICE
DIAMETER
0.24 IN (6 MM)

WEATHERED SURFACE
OF FOSSIL

*Alternating long
and short septa*

*Central boss
(protuberance)*

CORAL FACTS

• Growth lines on
fossil corals show
that years had 399
days during the
Devonian period.

• Colonies of *Galaxea*
can reach 52 feet
(16 meters) in diameter.

Scleractinians

All living corals, and their ancestors over
the past 230 million years, can be
distinguished from the older Paleozoic
corals by their six-fold pattern of
septal plates. Scleractinians include
both reef-forming and solitary
corals. The reef corals can reach
several yards in size, and are
restricted to shallow, tropical
waters. Smaller, solitary corals
can live at greater depths.

SEPTASTRAEA
Miocene–Pleistocene
This colonial reef-coral has many
clustered corallites. They can form a
wide variety of shapes
from branching to nodular.
The honeycomb-patterned
calices have 12
well-developed
septa that join at
a central point.

*Deep, thin-
walled calices*

TYPICAL CALICE DIAMETER
0.16 IN (4 MM)

TRACHYPHYLLIA
Miocene–Recent
This solitary coral lives
unattached on the seabed
in sheltered areas of soft sand.
The external wall is very thin and is
marked by fine growth ridges. Inside the
calice there are numerous septa, which
have serrated edges.

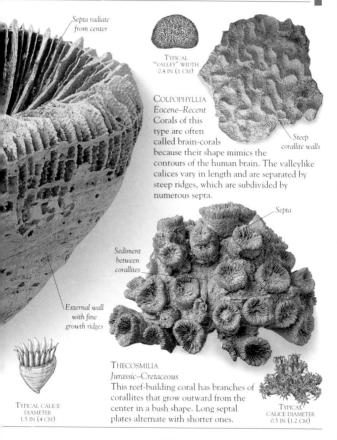

Septa radiate from center

TYPICAL "VALLEY" WIDTH
0.4 IN (1 CM)

COLPOPHYLLIA
Eocene–Recent
Corals of this
type are often
called brain-corals
because their shape mimics the
contours of the human brain. The valleylike
calices vary in length and are separated by
steep ridges, which are subdivided by
numerous septa.

Steep corallite walls

Septa

Sediment between corallites

External wall with fine growth ridges

TYPICAL CALICE
DIAMETER
1.5 IN (4 CM)

THECOSMILIA
Jurassic–Cretaceous
This reef-building coral has branches of
corallites that grow outward from the
center in a bush shape. Long septal
plates alternate with shorter ones.

TYPICAL
CALICE DIAMETER
0.5 IN (1.2 CM)

WORMS

SOFT-BODIED ANIMALS, such as worms, are not generally fossilized. However, their burrows in soil or sediment are often preserved as trace fossils – the only record of the worms' existence. Some worms line their burrows with a protective mineralized tube, and these are also found as trace fossils.

CHONDRITES
Triassic–Recent
This trace fossil consists only of sediment-filled worm burrows – no body parts are preserved. The pattern of the burrows seen here preserves a three-dimensional model of the worm's feeding activity.

Coiled tube

VARIABLE LENGTH

ROTULARIA
Eocene
These spiral fossils look like gastropod shells. In fact, they are the coiled, calcareous tubes of serpulid worms. The worms lived on soft sand in shallow seas, and built the tubes for protection against predators.

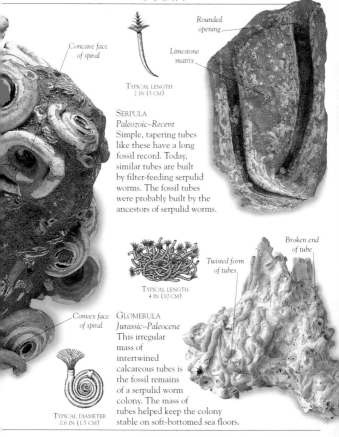

Concave face
of spiral

Rounded
opening

Limestone
matrix

TYPICAL LENGTH
2 IN (5 CM)

SERPULA
Paleozoic–Recent
Simple, tapering tubes
like these have a long
fossil record. Today,
similar tubes are built
by filter-feeding serpulid
worms. The fossil tubes
were probably built by the
ancestors of serpulid worms.

TYPICAL LENGTH
4 IN (10 CM)

Twisted form
of tubes

Broken end
of tube

Convex face
of spiral

GLOMERULA
Jurassic–Paleocene
This irregular
mass of
intertwined
calcareous tubes is
the fossil remains
of a serpulid worm
colony. The mass of
tubes helped keep the colony
stable on soft-bottomed sea floors.

TYPICAL DIAMETER
0.6 IN (1.5 CM)

BRACHIOPODS

THESE SMALL, SHELLED ANIMALS were the common shellfish in ancient seas. Brachiopods lived on the seabed and filtered food from the water. Since the beginning of the Mesozoic era, they have largely been replaced by bivalve mollusks.

Beak

SIDE-ON BRACHIOPOD
Most brachiopods can be distinguished from bivalve mollusks by the shape of their shells. One brachiopod valve (shell) is larger than the other and has a distinct "beak," often with a hole, at the base of the shell.

BRACHIOPOD FACTS
• There are more than 3,000 known genera of brachiopod, of which all but 100 are now extinct.
• The productids, a Carboniferous group of brachiopods, reached 15 in (38 cm) in width.

CYCLOTHYRIS
Cretaceous
A thin, fleshy stalk (pedicle) protruded from the hole in the beak of the larger shell, and anchored this brachiopod firmly to the sea bottom.

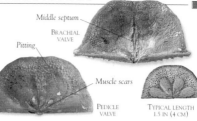

CHONETES
Permian
This small brachiopod was not attached to the seabed. The gently curved shells helped support it on soft mud. The hinge between the two shells is straight, and had a row of spines – now only the bases are visible.

Middle septum

BRACHIAL VALVE

Pitting

Muscle scars

PEDICLE VALVE

TYPICAL LENGTH 1.5 IN (4 CM)

Fold

Brachial valve

Sharp-crested ribs

TYPICAL WIDTH 1.2 IN (3 CM)

PLATYSTROPHIA
Ordovician
The shells are ribbed for strength and folded. The folding helped the animal maintain a constant current of food-bearing water between its two shells.

Deep fold

TYPICAL LENGTH 1.5 IN (4 CM)

PARAJURESANIA
Pennsylvanian
This fossil belongs to an extinct group of spiny brachiopods. The large lower shell is almost hemispherical, while the upper shell is flat and acts like a lid. The spines are rarely preserved.

Nearly erect spines

TYPICAL LENGTH 1.2 IN (3 CM)

BRYOZOANS

COLONIES OF TINY, interconnected bryozoan animals (zooids) make networks of calcareous tubes to live in. The bryozoans feed by filtering microorganisms from the surrounding seawater. Some colonies develop into upright, fan-shaped fronds. Others form flat networks, which spread out sideways, encrusting the surfaces of rocks, shells, pebbles, and seaweed.

OLD LACE
Chasmatopora, with delicate lacelike fronds, is one of the oldest bryozoan fossils, and dates from the Ordovician period.

Monticule

Tiny openings enabled bryozoan zooids to feed

TYPICAL LENGTH
0.8 IN (2 CM)

HIPPOPORIDRA
Miocene–Recent
This bryozoan grows on the surface of shells used by hermit crabs. Eventually the colony forms a thick crust of tiny, tightly packed tubes. Each tube houses an individual bryozoan zooid. Some zooids are clustered in small mounds called monticules.

Shell opening used by hermit crab

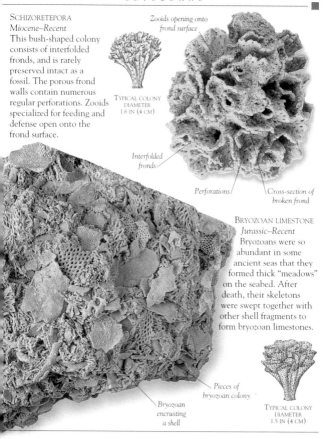

SCHIZORETEPORA
Miocene–Recent
This bush-shaped colony consists of interfolded fronds, and is rarely preserved intact as a fossil. The porous frond walls contain numerous regular perforations. Zooids specialized for feeding and defense open onto the frond surface.

Zooids opening onto frond surface

TYPICAL COLONY DIAMETER
1.6 IN (4 CM)

Interfolded fronds

Perforations

Cross-section of broken frond

BRYOZOAN LIMESTONE
Jurassic–Recent
Bryozoans were so abundant in some ancient seas that they formed thick "meadows" on the seabed. After death, their skeletons were swept together with other shell fragments to form bryozoan limestones.

Pieces of bryozoan colony

Bryozoan encrusting a shell

TYPICAL COLONY DIAMETER
1.5 IN (4 CM)

BIVALVES

THESE AQUATIC MOLLUSKS are enclosed and protected by two shells. Bivalves are abundant in shallow seas and their calcareous shells are commonly found as fossils. The shape and structure of the shell depends on the animal's way of life. By examining the shell, scientists can tell whether a fossil bivalve lived on the seabed or was suspended above the bottom.

Grooves made by hinge ligament

TYPICAL LENGTH
1.2 IN (3 CM)

Hinge teeth "lock" the two shells together

GLYCYMERIS
Cretaceous–Recent
Commonly known as the dog-cockle, this thick-shelled bivalve has a worldwide distribution. It can be recognized by a large triangular area grooved for the attachment of a ligament hinge.

GRYPHAEA
L. Triassic–L. Jurassic
This oysterlike bivalve has one large, coiled shell, which kept the animal upright on the seabed. A small upper shell fits inside like a lid.

Limestone matrix

Growth ridges

Concentric folds

Radial ribs

CARDIOLA
L. Silurian–Devonian
This extinct bivalve can be recognized by the rectangular pattern of ribs and concentric folds that strengthen its thin shells. Unlike most bivalves, *Cardiola* lacks the hinge teeth that help keep the two shells together.

TYPICAL LENGTH
0.6 IN (1.5 CM)

TYPICAL LENGTH
2.75 IN (7 CM)

AVICULOPECTEN
Mississippian–Permian
This fossil belongs to the widespread and successful scallop family. The animal's shell is attached to a firm surface by strong organic anchor-threads (byssus). The shell swings about in water currents like a wind vane while the animal filters food particles from the water.

Radial ribs

TYPICAL LENGTH
1 IN (2.5 CM)

GASTROPODS

FAMILIAR TODAY as garden slugs and snails, gastropods inhabit a wide variety of habitats: marine, freshwater, and terrestrial. Most gastropods are plant-eaters, and their fossils are frequently found in shallow-water deposits, where aquatic plants would have been most plentiful.

SHELL
EXTERIOR

Sunken inner coils

SHELL
EXTERIOR

AUSTRALORBIS
L. Cretaceous–Recent
Most gastropod shells coil to the right (dextrally). *Australorbis*, however, has a shell that coils to the left (sinistrally). The shell is thin, like that of most freshwater gastropods.

Regular inner coils

GASTROPOD FACTS
• More than 13,000 fossil species of gastropod have so far been discovered.

• Most gastropods are plant-eaters, but some marine species hunt other mollusks, and even small fish.

PLATYCERAS
Silurian–Mississippian
Fossils of this gastropod are sometimes found attached to crinoid cups. *Platyceras* shells are shaped to fit against the cups, and it is believed that the gastropod obtained its food from crinoids.

TYPICAL LENGTH
0.8 IN (2 CM)

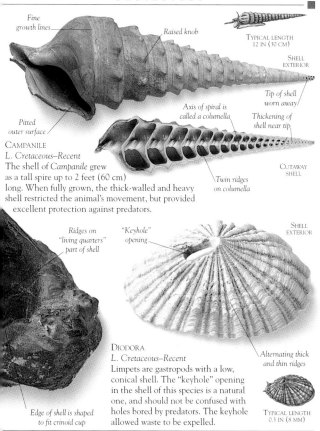

Fine growth lines

Raised knob

TYPICAL LENGTH
12 IN (30 CM)

SHELL
EXTERIOR

Tip of shell
worn away

Axis of spiral is
called a columella

Thickening of
shell near tip

Pitted
outer surface

CAMPANILE
L. Cretaceous–Recent
The shell of *Campanile* grew
as a tall spire up to 2 feet (60 cm)
long. When fully grown, the thick-walled and heavy
shell restricted the animal's movement, but provided
excellent protection against predators.

Twin ridges
on columella

CUTAWAY
SHELL

Ridges on
"living quarters"
part of shell

"Keyhole"
opening

SHELL
EXTERIOR

DIODORA
L. Cretaceous–Recent
Limpets are gastropods with a low,
conical shell. The "keyhole" opening
in the shell of this species is a natural
one, and should not be confused with
holes bored by predators. The keyhole
allowed waste to be expelled.

Alternating thick
and thin ridges

Edge of shell is shaped
to fit crinoid cup

TYPICAL LENGTH
0.3 IN (8 MM)

NAUTILOIDS

THESE SQUIDLIKE MOLLUSKS were abundant in Paleozoic seas. Early nautiloids had straight, conical shells. Later ones had shells that were tightly coiled. All the shells had chambers that were sealed off by internal walls as the animal grew bigger. Most nautiloids were swimming predators that used short tentacles to seize their prey.

CONNECTED CHAMBERS
A cross-section through a straight nautiloid shows how the chamber walls are connected by a central tube (siphuncle).

Fragments of original shell adhere to the internal mold

Rounded chamber wall

TYPICAL LENGTH
6 IN (15 CM)

ORTHOCERAS
M. Ordovician
This internal mold of a straight nautiloid shows numerous chambers. The curvature of the chamber walls can be seen at the rounded end of the fossil.

Uncoiled final coil

TYPICAL DIAMETER
4 IN (10 CM)

ESTONIOCERAS
E. Ordovician
This rare fossil is an internal mold of an early coiled nautiloid. The coils of the shell barely touch, and the final coil of this adult shell is partly uncoiled.

Numerous chambers

CENOCERAS
L. Triassic–M. Jurassic
A cross-section and internal mold of *Cenoceras* show how the later, adult coils grew over the juvenile coils, producing a tightly rolled shell. The living chamber is clearly visible at the open end. The smaller, older chambers were filled with gas, which helped the animal stay buoyant.

CROSS-SECTION

Mud-filled chambers

TYPICAL DIAMETER
6 IN (15 CM)

Broad, rounded shape

AMMONOIDS

THE DOMINANT MEMBERS of this group are the ammonites, which are related to the nautiloids. Ammonites have similar coiled and chambered shells. In ammonites, however, the siphuncle is near the edge of the shell, not in the center.

Complex and frilled chamber wall

TYPICAL DIAMETER
4 IN (10 CM)

PHYLLOCERAS
E. Jurassic–L. Cretaceous
This polished internal mold shows the complex folds of the internal chamber walls, which are a distinguishing feature of fossil ammonoids.

GASTRIOCERAS
Pennsylvanian
This ammonoid is known as a goniatite. The fossil internal mold shows that the folds of its chamber walls are more complex than those of a nautiloid, but not as complex as those of a true ammonite.

Calcite-filled chambers

TYPICAL DIAMETER
2.7 IN (7 CM)

Simple ribs of varying size

BOSTRYCHOCERAS
L. Cretaceous
This ammonite has a high, spired shell like some gastropods. It is thought to have been a poor swimmer, and to have drifted with ocean currents, hanging upright in the water.

TYPICAL HEIGHT
5.5 IN (14 CM)

Fine, closely spaced ribs

Apparently irregular coiling pattern

TYPICAL DIAMETER
2.4 IN (6 CM)

NIPPONITES
L. Cretaceous
The shell of this ammonite appears to be a disordered tangle of coils. In fact, it is a network of folded U-shapes. *Nipponites* is believed to have been planktonic – floating and drifting with ocean currents, rather than actually swimming.

Single opening

BELEMNITES

RELATED TO SQUID and cuttlefish, belemnites are extinct mollusks. Their remains consist largely of bullet-shaped fossils. These solid bullets were an internal "guard" that was used by the animal to regulate its buoyancy. Our knowledge of belemnite anatomy comes from a few rare fossils that preserve the soft parts.

BELEMNITE LIMESTONE
This polished limestone slab contains the remains of many belemnites. It is possible to see annual growth lines in one of the "bullets" that has been cut in half.

Calcite of belemnite guards

Concentric growth rings

BELEMNOTHEUTIS
This remarkable fossil has preserved the streamlined body outline of a belemnite. Some of the ten arms, or tentacles, can be seen extending from the head region. The tiny hooks on the arms enabled the belemnite to keep a firm grip on slippery prey.

Phragmocone sits in a cavity in the guard

TYPICAL LENGTH
9 IN (23 CM)

Chambered phragmocone

NEOHIBOLITES
Cretaceous
This belemnite was buried in a
fine-grained sediment, which has
preserved the delicate phragmocone
(a chambered internal shell) that lies in front of the
stony guard. Normally, the phragmocone is destroyed
by decay before the fossilization process can begin.

TRACHYTEUTHIS
L. Jurassic
This animal resembled the
living cuttlefish. Only the
flattened internal "cuttlebone,"
with clearly visible growth
lines, is preserved as a fossil.

Limestone

Flattened guard resembling cuttlebone

Growth lines on surface

TYPICAL LENGTH
10 IN (25 CM)

EARLY ARTHROPODS

THE APPEARANCE OF the early arthropods marked the end of the older, soft-bodied, Precambrian animals. Rigid arthropod exoskeletons and jointed appendages led to the development of jaws, which resulted in a wider range of feeding habits. The evidence for the diverse forms of early arthropods comes from a few sites with exceptional fossil preservation.

JIANFENGIA
E. Cambrian
This fossil is clearly an arthropod because of its exoskeleton and jointed legs. *Jianfengia* looks very like a crustacean, but it has been placed in a separate group.

MICRODICTYON
E. Cambrian
This caterpillar-like animal with a segmented body, paired legs, and spiny, armored plates is called a lobopod. It has characteristics that are midway between arthropods and worms.

TYPICAL LENGTH
2 IN (5 CM)

OPABINIA
E. Cambrian
Exceptional preservation shows that this segmented animal had a head with five eyes. Its most unusual characteristic is a single, long, flexible appendage attached to the head. This unique "trunk" was probably used to capture prey.

Forked tail

TYPICAL LENGTH
2.75 IN (7 CM)

Overlapping fleshy lobes

Appendage flattened against body

Marrella

CANADASPIS AND MARRELLA
E. Cambrian
These two fossils are the most common true arthropods in Canada's Burgess Shale deposits. *Canadaspis* (the larger animal) is the earliest known crustacean. The smaller *Marrella* is a trilobite-like animal.

Canadaspis

FOSSIL FACTS
• The Burgess Shale deposits have provided a greater range of arthropod fossils than any other site.

• The largest Burgess Shale fossil is of a 24-inch (60-cm) swimming predator called *Anomalocaris*.

TRILOBITES

THESE MARINE ARTHROPODS have a distinctive external skeleton. Separate head and tail shields are linked by a series of hinged plates. The upper part of the skeleton was mineralized with calcium carbonate to protect the soft body underneath. In order to grow, trilobites had to molt periodically. Many fossils are pieces of molted exoskeleton.

FOSSIL JEWELRY
Trilobites are very popular fossils. This well-preserved specimen of *Calymene* is more than 400 million years old. Sometime during the last century, its proud owner had it made into an attractive brooch.

ACADAGNOSTUS
M. *Cambrian*
This tiny trilobite is one of the agnostid group that lived in deep water. The head, which lacks eyes, and the tail are of similar size. The head and tail could fold together, hinged by the middle section.

TRILOBITE FACTS

• There are more than 1,500 trilobite genera.

• Agnostid trilobites swam with a flapping motion of their head and tail shields.

• As a group, trilobites survived for more than 350 million years.

Head shield

Tail shield

TYPICAL LENGTH
0.3 IN (8 MM)

PARADOXIDES
M. *Cambrian*
This is one of the largest trilobites, with some specimens reaching 39 inches (1 m) in length. The head shield has long spines at the sides, and the body is elongated.

Long thorax

TYPICAL
LENGTH
8 IN (20 CM)

Large eyes

XYSTRIDURA
M. *Cambrian*
This trilobite is similar to *Paradoxides* but has a shorter body with fewer segments. The position of the crescent-shaped eyes on the top of the head indicates that it lived on the seabed.

TYPICAL LENGTH
2.4 IN (6 CM)

Moderately large tail shield

Rolled trilobites

Fossil trilobites are sometimes found in a rolled-up (enrolled) position with the body plates flexed and the tail tucked under the head. Some could even lock the head and tail together, completely covering the legs and gills that protruded from the soft underpart of the body. It is most likely that they rolled themselves up for protection against predators.

ENROLLED SPECIMEN

PHACOPS
Devonian
Two features suggest that *Phacops* spent a lot of time avoiding predators. Large eyes enabled it to spot approaching enemies, and its body plates were modified for easy enrollment.

Tubercles on head

TYPICAL LENGTH
1.8 IN (4.5 CM)

Tubercular head shield

ENCRINURUS
L. Ordovician–Silurian
Fossil pieces of the molted skeleton of this trilobite are fairly common, but complete specimens are rare. *Encrinurus* is easily identified by the many distinctive tubercles (small raised lumps) on the head and large tail shield.

TYPICAL LENGTH
2.4 IN (6 CM)

Strong spine at side of head shield

HUNTONIA
This trilobite has well-developed spines for protection. Two long spines extend backward from the corners of the head shield. The animal also has a long tail spine, which has not been preserved in this fossil specimen.

Tail tucked beneath head when enrolled

LEONASPIS
Silurian–Devonian
This wide-bodied trilobite has small eyes and is fringed with protective spines. As well as spines on the head and tail shields, there are also spines on the body segments. *Leonaspis* fossils are very widely distributed around the world.

Downturned head shield

Paired tail-shield spines

TYPICAL LENGTH
0.6 IN (1.5 CM)

CRUSTACEANS

THE BODIES AND LIMBS of crustaceans are supported and protected by a tough external skeleton. In some species, the skeletons are reinforced by calcium carbonate, and these are the most common fossils. Like trilobites, most crustaceans have to molt their shells in order to grow.

TEALLIOCARIS
This shrimplike fossil is more than 300 million years old, but still preserves the delicate jointed legs and long antennae.

Outer pyramid of six plates

Inner pyramid of four plates

TYPICAL LENGTH
0.4 IN (1 CM)

Swimming paddle

BALANUS
Eocene–Recent
From the fossil remains alone, it is hard to tell that barnacles are in fact crustaceans. The pyramids of calcareous plates preserved in this fossil housed and protected a tiny shrimplike animal.

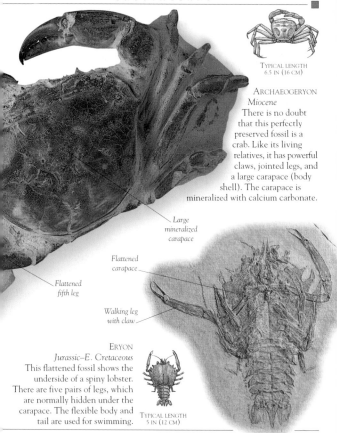

TYPICAL LENGTH
6.5 IN (16 CM)

ARCHAEOGERYON
Miocene
There is no doubt
that this perfectly
preserved fossil is a
crab. Like its living
relatives, it has powerful
claws, jointed legs, and
a large carapace (body
shell). The carapace is
mineralized with calcium carbonate.

Large
mineralized
carapace

Flattened
carapace

Walking leg
with claw

Flattened
fifth leg

ERYON
Jurassic–E. Cretaceous
This flattened fossil shows the
underside of a spiny lobster.
There are five pairs of legs, which
are normally hidden under the
carapace. The flexible body and
tail are used for swimming.

TYPICAL LENGTH
5 IN (12 CM)

INSECTS AND SPIDERS

JOINTED LEGS AND EXOSKELETONS identify insects and spiders as arthropods. Well adapted for life on land, they inhabit every terrestrial habitat from tundra to desert. During the past 350 million years, insects have become the most abundant animals on Earth. However, their fossils are quite rare because their exoskeletons are not mineralized.

BIBIO
This fly was preserved next to a leaf in a block of freshwater limestone. The insect can be recognized as a true fly by the large head and pattern of veins on its transparent wings.

INSECT FACTS

• The largest known insect is *Megatypus*, a 300-million-year-old dragonfly with a wing span of nearly 39 inches (1 m).

• The first known insect is a 400-million-year-old springtail.

ARCHIMYLACRIS
Pennsylvanica
Cockroaches are one of the oldest groups of insects and have changed very little through time. This fossil cockroach is more than 300 million years old. It is identifiable by the strengthened forewings that fold over the hindwings.

Ironstone

Thorax

TYPICAL LENGTH
0.8 IN (2 CM)

Hindwing

7 6

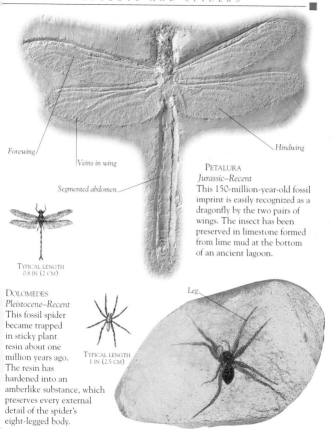

Forewing

Veins in wing

Segmented abdomen

Hindwing

PETALURA
Jurassic–Recent
This 150-million-year-old fossil imprint is easily recognized as a dragonfly by the two pairs of wings. The insect has been preserved in limestone formed from lime mud at the bottom of an ancient lagoon.

TYPICAL LENGTH
0.8 IN (2 CM)

DOLOMEDES
Pleistocene–Recent
This fossil spider became trapped in sticky plant resin about one million years ago. The resin has hardened into an amberlike substance, which preserves every external detail of the spider's eight-legged body.

TYPICAL LENGTH
1 IN (2.5 CM)

Leg

SEA STARS

STARFISH AND BRITTLE STARS are related to sea urchins, and have a similar five-fold structure. Their flexible arms are composed of small calcareous ossicles (small plates). Starfish are highly mobile, and many are active predators of shellfish. Fossil sea stars are rarely preserved intact, but jumbled piles of fossilized ossicles occur quite frequently.

STENASTER
The original skeleton of this starfish has dissolved over 400 million years. The shape is preserved as a mold in a block of sandstone.

Ridge formed by ossicles

TYPICAL DIAMETER
5 IN (12 CM)

PALASTERICUS
L. Devonian
The broad arms of this starfish helped prevent it from sinking into soft, seabed mud. The original skeleton of small ossicles and spines has here been preserved in iron pyrites.

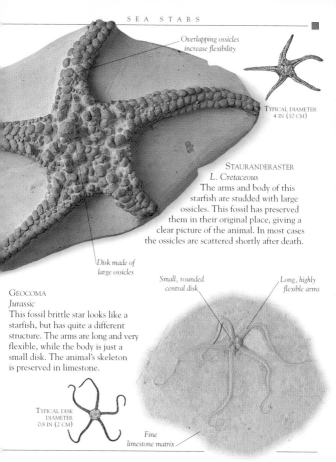

Overlapping ossicles
increase flexibility

TYPICAL DIAMETER
4 IN (10 CM)

STAURANDERASTER
L. Cretaceous
The arms and body of this
starfish are studded with large
ossicles. This fossil has preserved
them in their original place, giving a
clear picture of the animal. In most cases
the ossicles are scattered shortly after death.

Disk made of
large ossicles

Small, rounded
central disk

Long, highly
flexible arms

GEOCOMA
Jurassic
This fossil brittle star looks like a
starfish, but has quite a different
structure. The arms are long and very
flexible, while the body is just a
small disk. The animal's skeleton
is preserved in limestone.

TYPICAL DISK
DIAMETER
0.8 IN (2 CM)

Fine
limestone matrix

SEA URCHINS

THE FOSSIL HISTORY of sea urchins (echinoids) dates back to Ordovician times. Echinoids have skeletons made of five-fold rows of calcareous plates with pores between them. Spines are used both for movement and defense. Complete fossils are fairly rare since the skeletons fall apart after death, leaving just separated plates and spines.

HEMICIDARIS
Sea urchins with nearly spherical shells are called regular echinoids. The fact that the spines are still attached means that the urchin was buried in sediment soon after death.

SEA URCHIN FACTS
• Echinoderm means "spiny skin." Crystals of calcium carbonate are held together by a thin layer of tissue.

• Irregular sea urchins do not appear in the fossil record until the Jurassic period.

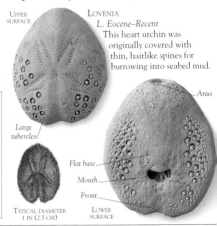

UPPER SURFACE

LOVENIA
L. Eocene–Recent
This heart urchin was originally covered with thin, hairlike spines for burrowing into seabed mud.

Anus

Large tubercles

Flat base

Mouth

Front

TYPICAL DIAMETER
1 IN (2.5 CM)

LOWER SURFACE

Tiny tubercles

TYPICAL
DIAMETER
5 IN (12 CM)

*Rows of pores
used for respiration*

CLYPEASTER
L. Eocene–Recent
With its flattened shape, this is
an irregular echinoid. When
living, it was covered with
small spines that helped it
to burrow into soft sediment.
The five-fold structure of the
skeleton is made clearly visible
by the petal-shaped rows of
pores on the upper surface.

TYLOCIDARIS
L. Cretaceous–Eocene
This regular echinoid had remarkable
club-shaped spines for defense. The spines
are rarely still attached to the skeleton,
but are often
found separately
as fossils.

TYPICAL DIAMETER
1.2 IN (3 CM)

*Large, club-
shaped spines*

*Large tubercles
between plates*

Underside

*Position of
mouth opening*

SEA LILIES

NOT PLANTS but animals, sea lilies (crinoids) are related to sea urchins and sea stars, and have a similar five-fold structure. Many have long, flexible stems rooted in the seabed. At the top of the stem is a cup and feathery arms. The cups are made of calcareous plates held together by skin.

Globular cup

Branched arms

CYATHOCRINITES
This fossil preserves only the top of the crinoid. Five arms extend upward from a small cup. The arms divide to produce a many-branched, bushy crown made of numerous small plates.

TYPICAL CUP DIAMETER
0.8 IN (2 CM)

SACCOCOMA
L. *Jurassic*
This small and delicate crinoid has ten long, feathery arms. These were used both for swimming and for capturing microscopic food particles.

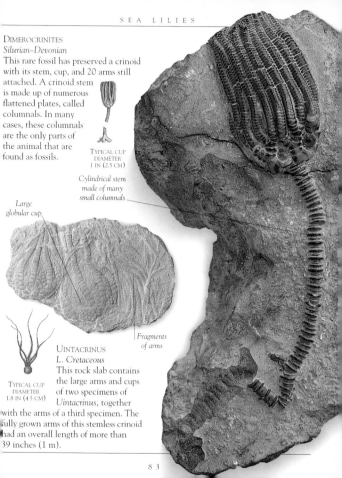

DIMEROCRINITES
Silurian–Devonian
This rare fossil has preserved a crinoid with its stem, cup, and 20 arms still attached. A crinoid stem is made up of numerous flattened plates, called columnals. In many cases, these columnals are the only parts of the animal that are found as fossils.

TYPICAL CUP DIAMETER
1 IN (2.5 CM)

Cylindrical stem made of many small columnals

Large globular cup

Fragments of arms

TYPICAL CUP DIAMETER
1.8 IN (4.5 CM)

UINTACRINUS
L. Cretaceous
This rock slab contains the large arms and cups of two specimens of *Uintacrinus*, together with the arms of a third specimen. The fully grown arms of this stemless crinoid had an overall length of more than 39 inches (1 m).

GRAPTOLITES

THESE EXTINCT COLONIAL animals are
common fossils in old sedimentary
rocks. Some graptolite colonies
grew attached to the seabed, but
most floated with the ocean
currents. Each colony built an
organic skeleton consisting of
linked thecae (cups). These
skeletons are often preserved
as flattened fossils.

LOGANOGRAPTUS
E. Ordovician
This graptolite colony has
been preserved in a red shale
that stands out against the
surrounding gray. During
fossilization, the 16 radial
branches became twisted,
revealing the flattened thecae.

*Spirally
branched
colony*

CYRTOGRAPTUS
Silurian
Graptolites got their name
because some graptolite fossils
look like disjointed writing in the
rock surface. This colony originally
had a spiral form, but fossilization
has distorted the shape.

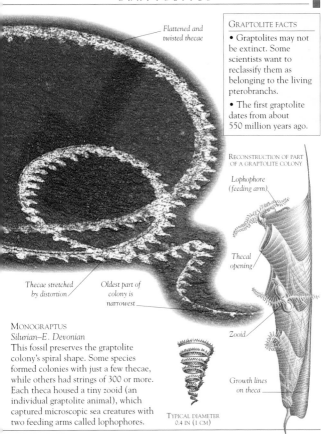

Flattened and twisted thecae

GRAPTOLITE FACTS

• Graptolites may not be extinct. Some scientists want to reclassify them as belonging to the living pterobranchs.

• The first graptolite dates from about 550 million years ago.

RECONSTRUCTION OF PART OF A GRAPTOLITE COLONY

Lophophore (feeding arm)

Thecal opening

Thecae stretched by distortion

Oldest part of colony is narrowest

Zooid

Growth lines on theca

MONOGRAPTUS
Silurian–E. Devonian
This fossil preserves the graptolite colony's spiral shape. Some species formed colonies with just a few thecae, while others had strings of 300 or more. Each theca housed a tiny zooid (an individual graptolite animal), which captured microscopic sea creatures with two feeding arms called lophophores.

TYPICAL DIAMETER
0.4 IN (1 CM)

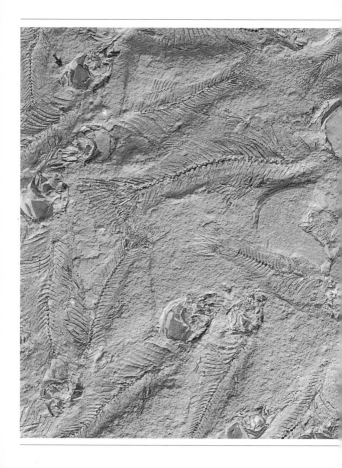

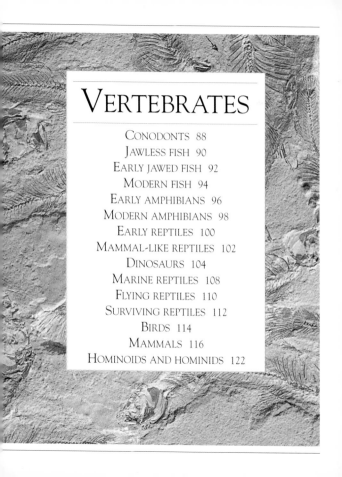

VERTEBRATES

CONODONTS

SMALL FOSSIL TEETH (conodonts) have been found in large numbers but, for more than 100 years, they were a mystery. Only recently have fossils been discovered that show the whole of the conodont animal. Conodonts are important because they are thought to have come from the earliest vertebrate animals.

TEETH AND EYES
This remarkable fossil contains the eyes and toothed feeding apparatus of the largest known conodont animal. The living animal was some 16 inches (40 cm) long. Near the eyes (black circles), are preserved the remains of some eye muscles, which are unique to vertebrates.

MICROSCOPIC TEETH
These two scanning electron micrographs show examples of conodonts. The wear marks on the teeth show that conodont animals were predators.

Saw-edged tooth blade

Microscopic wear marks indicate a diet of meat

Grains of matrix (rock)

DISSOLVED OUT OF ROCK
Like all vertebrate teeth, conodont teeth are made of calcium phosphate. They can be extracted from the matrix by dissolving the rock with powerful acids. These teeth still have some grains of matrix attached.

TEETH RECONSTRUCTION
This plastic model is a
reconstruction that shows
how the teeth were
arranged in the animal's
mouth. The forward-
pointing and curved teeth
(yellow) were used for
seizing and holding the
prey. The scissorlike teeth
(red) sliced up food.

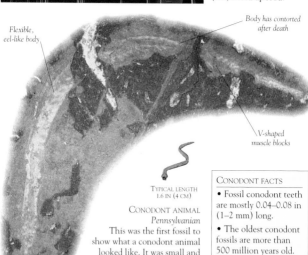

*Flexible,
eel-like body*

*Body has contorted
after death*

*V-shaped
muscle blocks*

TYPICAL LENGTH
1.6 IN (4 CM)

CONODONT ANIMAL
Pennsylvanian
This was the first fossil to
show what a conodont animal
looked like. It was small and
eel-like, with large eyes and a
mouth full of teeth. Normally
only the scattered teeth are
preserved as fossils.

CONODONT FACTS

• Fossil conodont teeth
are mostly 0.04–0.08 in
(1–2 mm) long.

• The oldest conodont
fossils are more than
500 million years old.

• Conodont animals
became extinct about
200 million years ago.

JAWLESS FISH

THE FIRST FISH were jawless (agnathan) and probably
sucked food directly from seawater and sediment.
Agnathans swam in great numbers in shallow seas
during the Silurian period. During the Devonian
period, they entered freshwater environments.
Fossil agnathans may be related to modern
jawless fish, such as lampreys.

BIRKENIA
M. *Silurian*
This is one of the more typically fishlike of the extinct
agnathans. It is covered with small, thin, overlapping
scales that allowed the animal to swim by flexing
its body from
side to side.

*Long, spindle-
shaped body*

*Bony plates
cover head*

*Rows of
scales*

TYPICAL LENGTH 2.4 IN (6 CM)

CEPHALASPIS
E. Devonian

Like many extinct agnathans, *Cephalaspis* had a strong, bony head shield. The eyes are on the top of the head, and the mouth on the underside. These features suggest that *Cephalaspis* lived on river bottoms.

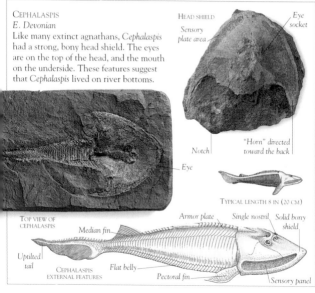

HEAD SHIELD

Sensory plate area

Eye socket

Notch

"Horn" directed toward the back

Eye

TYPICAL LENGTH 8 IN (20 CM)

TOP VIEW OF CEPHALASPIS

Median fin

Armor plate — Single nostril — Solid bony shield

Uptilted tail

CEPHALASPIS EXTERNAL FEATURES

Flat belly — Pectoral fin

Sensory panel

PTERASPIS
E. Devonian

Immovable side plate

This bizarre agnathan has a cylindrical head shield with a spine at the back and a prominent snout. The fish swam by using its tail alone and the snout gave lift to its body.

TYPICAL LENGTH 10 IN (25 CM)

EARLY JAWED FISH

AFTER THE DEVELOPMENT of jaws, fish went through many changes in shape and structure. Some had plated, armored bodies, and some had cartilaginous skeletons like modern sharks. Others had internal bony skeletons. Many types are now extinct.

Head shield

BOTHRIOLEPIS
L. Devonian
The head, body, and "arms" (pectoral appendages) are all encased in bony plates. The "arms" were probably used to provide lift and balance. Only the tail was used for swimming.

Long pectoral appendage

TYPICAL LENGTH 16 IN (40 CM)

TYPICAL LENGTH 12 IN (30 CM)

CHEIRACANTHUS
Devonian
The jaws and fin-supporting spines can be seen in this flattened fossil fish. The spines also provided some protection to the body that was otherwise covered in small scales.

Scale-covered body

Dorsal fin

TYPICAL LENGTH 6 IN (15 CM)

Notched
tail fin

DICELLOPYGE
E. Triassic
This freshwater fish is
streamlined, and its body is
covered with small diamond-
shaped, overlapping scales. It had
big eyes, long jaws, and sharp teeth.
These features suggest *Dicellopyge* was
probably a predator that fed on smaller fish.

Large
mature teeth

ESTIMATED LENGTH
12 FT (3.5 M)

Small
juvenile teeth

HELICOPRION
E. Permian
This teeth of this extinct shark
grew in a spiral. There are up to
180 teeth in the spiral. They
range from small, juvenile teeth
at the center of the spiral to
large, worn-out teeth in
the outermost coil.

Scale-covered
body

MODERN FISH

MODERN JAWED FISH are mostly ray-finned fishes with internal, bony skeletons or sharklike fishes with cartilaginous skeletons. The bony fish are much more commonly found as fossils. Cartilage does not normally fossilize, and usually the teeth are the only part of sharks that are preserved.

Vertebral column

DIPLOMYSTUS
Cretaceous–Eocene
This well-preserved freshwater fish has a distinctive upturned mouth. The shape and position of the mouth indicate that the fish was a surface feeder.

Upturned mouth

TYPICAL LENGTH
8.5 IN (21 CM)

PRISCACARA
Eocene
This freshwater fish was a slow swimmer, and probably ate small invertebrates (snails and crustaceans) that lived on river or lake beds.

Lower jaw   TYPICAL LENGTH 6 IN (15 CM)

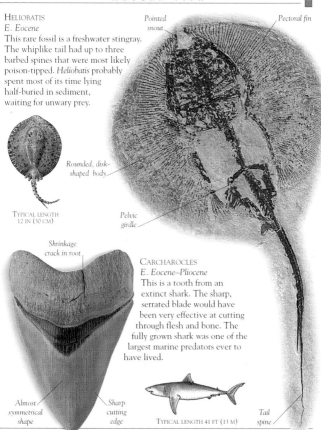

HELIOBATIS
E. Eocene
This rare fossil is a freshwater stingray. The whiplike tail had up to three barbed spines that were most likely poison-tipped. *Heliobatis* probably spent most of its time lying half-buried in sediment, waiting for unwary prey.

Pointed snout

Pectoral fin

Rounded, disk-shaped body

TYPICAL LENGTH 12 IN (30 CM)

Pelvic girdle

Shrinkage crack in root

CARCHAROCLES
E. Eocene–Pliocene
This is a tooth from an extinct shark. The sharp, serrated blade would have been very effective at cutting through flesh and bone. The fully grown shark was one of the largest marine predators ever to have lived.

Almost symmetrical shape

Sharp cutting edge

TYPICAL LENGTH 41 FT (13 M)

Tail spine

95

EARLY AMPHIBIANS

THE FIRST TETRAPODS (four-legged animals) to walk on land were amphibians. Distantly related to modern amphibians, they looked rather like large newts or salamanders. Although amphibians can breathe air through lungs and move about freely on land, they must return to an aquatic habitat in order to reproduce.

Nostrils

Pit and ridge ornament

BATRACHOSUCHUS
Triassic
The skull of this
extinct amphibian
is made up of bony plates. The
position of the eyes and nostrils at
the front of the skull suggests that
the animal spent most of its time
swimming at the surface.

TYPICAL LENGTH
20 IN (50 CM)

*Very thick bones at
the top of the skull*

PERMIAN PREDATOR
This skeleton of *Eryops* is
nearly 6 feet (2 m) long.
The mouth full
of sharp teeth
indicates that
Eryops was
a meat-
eater. It
probably
hunted its prey
near lakes and rivers.

*Sharp teeth of
a meat-eater*

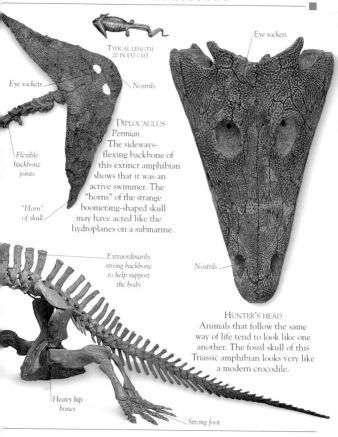

TYPICAL LENGTH
20 IN (50 CM)

Eye sockets

Nostrils

Eye sockets

Flexible
backbone
joints

"Horn"
of skull

DIPLOCAULUS
Permian
The sideways-
flexing backbone of
this extinct amphibian
shows that it was an
active swimmer. The
"horns" of the strange
boomerang-shaped skull
may have acted like the
hydroplanes on a submarine.

Extraordinarily
strong backbone
to help support
the body

Nostrils

HUNTER'S HEAD
Animals that follow the same
way of life tend to look like one
another. The fossil skull of this
Triassic amphibian looks very like
a modern crocodile.

Heavy hip
bones

Strong foot

MODERN AMPHIBIANS

MODERN AMPHIBIANS and their fossil ancestors are a very varied group of animals, but most lay jellylike eggs in water. These eggs hatch into tadpolelike larvae that later metamorphose into the adult form. Modern amphibians (frogs, toads, salamanders, and caecilians) inhabit exclusively freshwater and terrestrial environments. As a result, they are not often preserved, and their fossils are quite rare.

FOSSIL TADPOLE
The body outline and even the eyes are preserved in this exceptional fossil. The tadpole has no legs, which indicates an early stage of development.

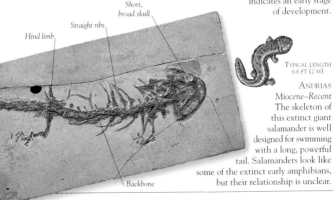

Short, broad skull

Straight ribs

Hind limb

Backbone

TYPICAL LENGTH
6.6 FT (2 M)

ANDRIAS
Miocene–Recent
The skeleton of this extinct giant salamander is well designed for swimming with a long, powerful tail. Salamanders look like some of the extinct early amphibians, but their relationship is unclear.

RANA
Eocene–Recent
There is no mistaking this fossil frog, with its
pointed skull and shock-absorbing shoulder
bones. Traces of the soft parts
of the body, as well as the
skeleton, are preserved.
The muscular hind
limbs are well
adapted for
swimming
and jumping.

AMPHIBIAN FACTS
• The oldest known
frog is *Triadobatrachus*,
from early in the
Triassic period.
• Amphibians were the
first vertebrates to walk
on land more than
380 million years ago.

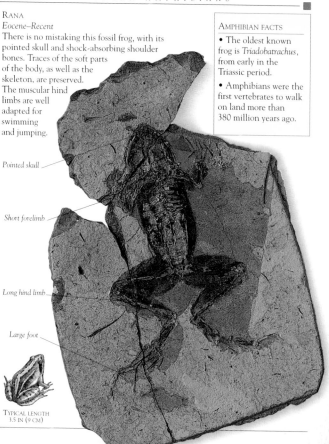

Pointed skull

Short forelimb

Long hind limb

Large foot

TYPICAL LENGTH
3.5 IN (9 CM)

EARLY REPTILES

THE FIRST REPTILES appeared during the Pennsylvanian period, long before the dinosaurs. There was a great variety of these now-extinct reptiles. They ranged from small lizardlike animals to bulky plant-eaters up to 13 feet (4 meters) long. Reptiles are classified according to the number of openings in their skulls.

Triangular skull

Forelimb

Ribs

Spinal vertebra

PROCOLOPHON
E. Triassic
The thick-boned limbs of this small, plant-eating reptile gave it a slow, ambling gait. The short skull has rows of peg teeth on both jaws and along the roof of the mouth.

Hind limb

Tail

TYPICAL LENGTH
13 IN (33 CM)

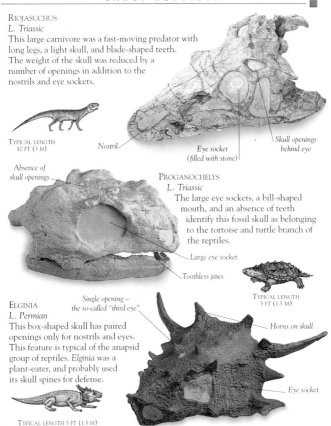

RIOJASUCHUS
L. Triassic
This large carnivore was a fast-moving predator with long legs, a light skull, and blade-shaped teeth. The weight of the skull was reduced by a number of openings in addition to the nostrils and eye sockets.

TYPICAL LENGTH
10 FT (3 M)

Nostril

Eye socket
(filled with stone)

Skull openings
behind eye

Absence of
skull openings

PROGANOCHELYS
L. Triassic
The large eye sockets, a bill-shaped mouth, and an absence of teeth identify this fossil skull as belonging to the tortoise and turtle branch of the reptiles.

Large eye socket

Toothless jaws

TYPICAL LENGTH
5 FT (1.5 M)

Single opening –
the so-called "third eye"

ELGINIA
L. Permian
This box-shaped skull has paired openings only for nostrils and eyes. This feature is typical of the anapsid group of reptiles. *Elginia* was a plant-eater, and probably used its skull spines for defense.

Horns on skull

Eye socket

TYPICAL LENGTH 5 FT (1.5 M)

MAMMAL-LIKE REPTILES

THIS EXTRAORDINARY GROUP of extinct reptiles had a number of mammal-like features. During the Permian period, they were the most successful land animals. Other reptiles, especially the dinosaurs, later took over. After giving rise to the true mammals, the mammal-like reptiles became extinct during Jurassic times.

Eye socket

Incisors

TYPICAL LENGTH
6.5 FT (2 M)

BIENOTHERIUM
E. Jurassic
The mammal-like feature in this skull is the difference between the peglike incisors (front teeth) and the squarer chewing teeth in the cheeks.

REPTILE FACTS

• The oldest known mammal-like reptile is *Archaeothyris*, found in rocks of the Pennsylvanian period.

• Some mammal-like reptiles were almost certainly warm-blooded.

Eye socket

Nostril

SINOKANNEMEYERIA
E. Triassic
This large animal had a heavily boned skull, a bill-like mouth, and side tusks. Like most heavily built animals, it was a plant-eater. It depended on its bulk, massive skull, and tusks for self-defense.

Wrist joint

DIMETRODON
E. Permian

Dagger-shaped teeth show that *Dimetrodon* was a meat-eater. The sail on its back probably helped the animal regulate its internal temperature.

TYPICAL LENGTH
10 FT (3 M)

Nostril

Eye socket

Daggerlike teeth

Jaw articulation

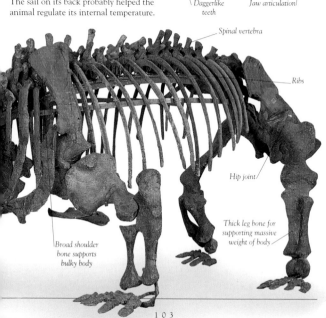

Spinal vertebra

Ribs

Hip joint

Thick leg bone for supporting massive weight of body

Broad shoulder bone supports bulky body

DINOSAURS

FOR SOME 250 MILLION years,
dinosaurs were the dominant
land animals. They ranged
in size from two-legged meat-
eaters the size of a chicken to
giant, four-footed plant-eaters.
Their fossils are usually found
as scattered, and often broken,
bones in sediments from ancient
rivers and lakes. Complete
dinosaur skeletons are
extremely rare.

Cheek teeth for
chewing plants

Forelimb folded
beneath neck

COMPSOGNATHUS
L. Jurassic
   This is one of the smallest
known dinosaurs, no larger
than a domestic chicken. Its fossil
skeleton is very similar to that of
Archaeopteryx, one of the first birds.
Compsognathus was a meat-eater that
hunted insects and lizards.

Tail vertebra

Head

Eye socket

Long hind limb

Forelimb

TYPICAL LENGTH 24 IN (60 CM)

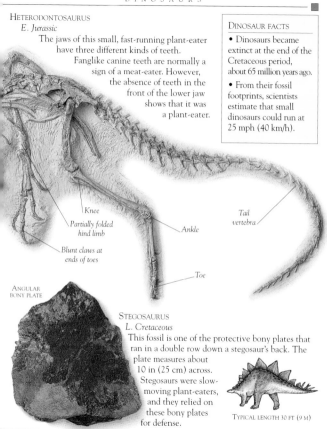

HETERODONTOSAURUS
E. Jurassic
The jaws of this small, fast-running plant-eater have three different kinds of teeth. Fanglike canine teeth are normally a sign of a meat-eater. However, the absence of teeth in the front of the lower jaw shows that it was a plant-eater.

DINOSAUR FACTS

• Dinosaurs became extinct at the end of the Cretaceous period, about 65 million years ago.

• From their fossil footprints, scientists estimate that small dinosaurs could run at 25 mph (40 km/h).

Knee

Partially folded hind limb

Ankle

Blunt claws at ends of toes

Tail vertebra

Toe

ANGULAR BONY PLATE

STEGOSAURUS
L. Cretaceous
This fossil is one of the protective bony plates that ran in a double row down a stegosaur's back. The plate measures about 10 in (25 cm) across. Stegosaurs were slow-moving plant-eaters, and they relied on these bony plates for defense.

TYPICAL LENGTH 30 FT (9 M)

Dinosaur types

Dinosaurs can be divided into a number of groups. The most basic distinction is the one between the saurischian ("lizard-hipped") dinosaurs, and the ornithischian ("bird-hipped") dinosaurs. The saurischian group included gigantic sauropods, such as *Diplodocus*, and ferocious hunters like *Tyrannosaurus*. The ornithischian group included the crested hadrosaurs, stegosaurs, and horned ceratopsians.

Tail held rigid by bony rods

PARASAUROLOPHUS
L. Cretaceous
This fossil hadrosaur skull shows the hollow, bony crest, which the animal probably used to amplify warning or mating calls.

SKULL

Frill

PROTOCERATOPS
L. Cretaceous
This skull shows two of the most prominent characteristics of the ceratopsian group of dinosaurs: a horny beak and a frill at the back of the head. The first dinosaur nests to be discovered contained *Protoceratops* eggs.

Roof of skull

Eye socket

Upper jaw

TYPICAL LENGTH 6 FT (1.8 M)

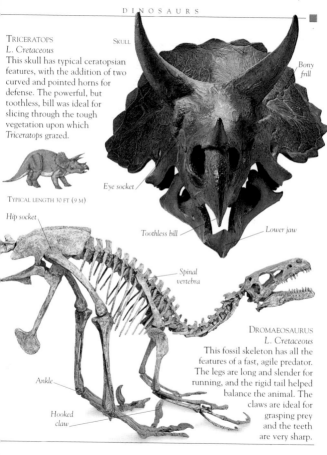

TRICERATOPS
L. Cretaceous
This skull has typical ceratopsian features, with the addition of two curved and pointed horns for defense. The powerful, but toothless, bill was ideal for slicing through the tough vegetation upon which *Triceratops* grazed.

SKULL

Bony frill

Eye socket

TYPICAL LENGTH 30 FT (9 M)

Toothless bill

Lower jaw

Hip socket

Spinal vertebra

DROMAEOSAURUS
L. Cretaceous
This fossil skeleton has all the features of a fast, agile predator. The legs are long and slender for running, and the rigid tail helped balance the animal. The claws are ideal for grasping prey and the teeth are very sharp.

Ankle

Hooked claw

MARINE REPTILES

MOST REPTILES lay eggs and live on land. The fossil record, however, shows that in the past many reptiles lived in water. These aquatic reptiles were all meat-eaters, hunting fish and invertebrates. Some fossils suggest that ichthyosaurs may have given birth in the water to live young.

Skull openings behind eye sockets

TYPICAL LENGTH
12 IN (30 CM)

METRIORHYNCHUS
M.–L. Jurassic
The long, narrow skull of this marine crocodile is streamlined for fast swimming in pursuit of fish and belemnites. The openings in the skull behind the eye sockets are much larger in marine crocodiles than in terrestrial ones. This feature probably allowed the jaws to gape widely.

FISH LIZARDS
The most remarkable of the marine reptiles were the ichthyosaurs (fish-lizards). Well adapted to hunting in the open seas, they are similar in size and shape to modern dolphins.

Tail bones have a distinctive downward kink

Remnants of hind limbs

Paddle (forelimb) for steering

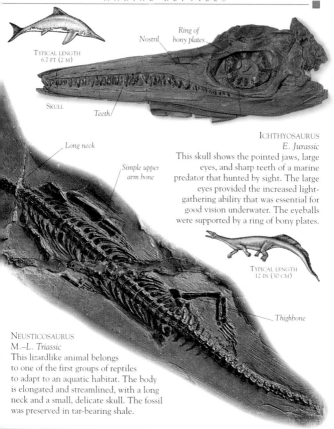

TYPICAL LENGTH
6.7 FT (2 M)

SKULL

Nostril

Ring of
bony plates

Teeth

ICHTHYOSAURUS
E. Jurassic
This skull shows the pointed jaws, large
eyes, and sharp teeth of a marine
predator that hunted by sight. The large
eyes provided the increased light-
gathering ability that was essential for
good vision underwater. The eyeballs
were supported by a ring of bony plates.

TYPICAL LENGTH
12 IN (30 CM)

Long neck

Simple upper
arm bone

Thighbone

NEUSTICOSAURUS
M.–L. Triassic
This lizardlike animal belongs
to one of the first groups of reptiles
to adapt to an aquatic habitat. The body
is elongated and streamlined, with a long
neck and a small, delicate skull. The fossil
was preserved in tar-bearing shale.

FLYING REPTILES

THE EXTINCT PTEROSAURS were the only group of reptiles to successfully conquer the air through powered flight. Pterosaurs were probably warm-blooded, and some were definitely covered with fine hair. During the Mesozoic era, they had little competition from birds and were mainly fish-eaters. They varied greatly in size; most were quite small, but some were far larger than any bird.

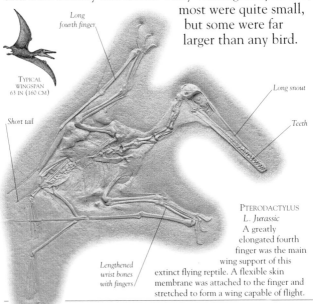

Long
fourth finger

TYPICAL
WINGSPAN
63 IN (160 CM)

Long snout

Short tail

Teeth

PTERODACTYLUS
L. Jurassic
A greatly
elongated fourth
finger was the main
wing support of this
extinct flying reptile. A flexible skin
membrane was attached to the finger and
stretched to form a wing capable of flight.

Lengthened
wrist bones
with fingers

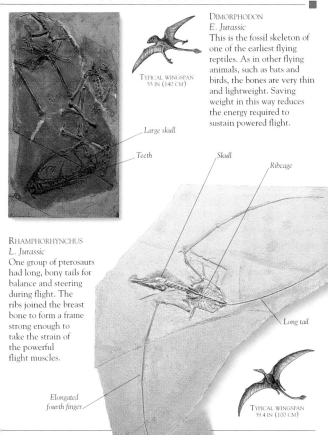

DIMORPHODON
E. Jurassic
This is the fossil skeleton of one of the earliest flying reptiles. As in other flying animals, such as bats and birds, the bones are very thin and lightweight. Saving weight in this way reduces the energy required to sustain powered flight.

TYPICAL WINGSPAN
55 IN (140 CM)

Large skull

Teeth

Skull

Ribcage

RHAMPHORHYNCHUS
L. Jurassic
One group of pterosaurs had long, bony tails for balance and steering during flight. The ribs joined the breast bone to form a frame strong enough to take the strain of the powerful flight muscles.

Long tail

Elongated fourth finger

TYPICAL WINGSPAN
39.4 IN (100 CM)

SURVIVING REPTILES

THE DOMINANCE of the reptiles ended with the extinction of the dinosaurs, but there are still more reptile species than mammal species. Crocodiles, lizards, tortoises, turtles, and snakes all survived to the present day. Of these groups, crocodiles are the most ancient and snakes the most recent.

Large eye socket

TYPICAL LENGTH
10 FT (3 M)

DINILYSIA
L. Cretaceous
This fossil skull shows several features typical of land snakes. The eye sockets are large, and the jaws are loosely hinged so they can open wide.

Eye socket

Broad snout

DIPLOCYNODON
Eocene–Pliocene
The crocodiles are a remarkable group that has survived from the Triassic period. They now form three families: true crocodiles, gavials, and alligators. This skull belonged to a medium-sized alligator.

Nostrils

TYPICAL LENGTH
10 FT (3 M)

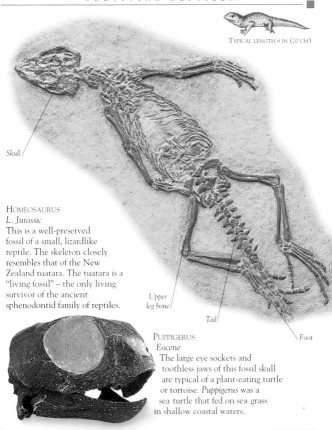

TYPICAL LENGTH 8 IN (20 CM)

Skull

HOMEOSAURUS
L. Jurassic
This is a well-preserved
fossil of a small, lizardlike
reptile. The skeleton closely
resembles that of the New
Zealand tuatara. The tuatara is a
"living fossil" – the only living
survivor of the ancient
sphenodontid family of reptiles.

Upper
leg bone

Tail

Foot

PUPPIGERUS
Eocene
The large eye sockets and
toothless jaws of this fossil skull
are typical of a plant-eating turtle
or tortoise. *Puppigerus* was a
sea turtle that fed on sea grass
in shallow coastal waters.

BIRDS

THERE ARE MORE species of bird today than either reptiles or mammals. During the past 60 million years, birds have become extremely varied in size, shape, and lifestyle. They are, however, very rare as fossils because their lightweight bones do not preserve well. The earliest known bird is *Archaeopteryx*, which has many dinosaur-like characteristics.

TYPICAL HEIGHT
OF ADULT BIRD
10 FT (3 M)

AEPYORNIS
Pleistocene–Recent
This egg is larger than most dinosaur eggs, and has a capacity of about 2 gallons (8.5 liters). It was laid by a giant, flightless, ostrichlike bird.

RAPHUS
Quaternary
This is the fossil skull of a Mauritian dodo, which only became extinct during the seventeenth century. The dodo was a large, flightless pigeon that was wiped out by humans. Only some fossils and a few stuffed specimens remain.

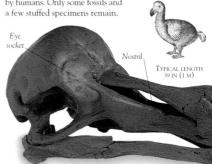

Eye socket

Nostril

TYPICAL LENGTH
39 IN (1 M)

BIRD FACTS

• Only about 1,000 fossil bird species have been found, compared with more than 9,000 living species.

• The heaviest bird ever was *Aepyornis*, which weighed about 970 lb (440 kg).

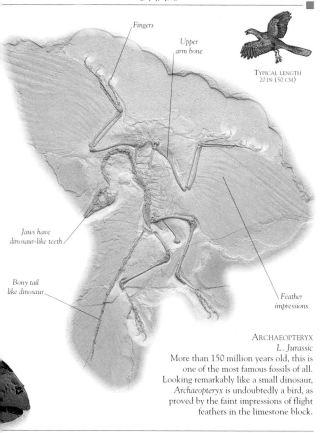

Fingers

Upper
arm bone

TYPICAL LENGTH
20 IN (50 CM)

Jaws have
dinosaur-like teeth

Bony tail
like dinosaur

Feather
impressions

ARCHAEOPTERYX
L. Jurassic
More than 150 million years old, this is
one of the most famous fossils of all.
Looking remarkably like a small dinosaur,
Archaeopteryx is undoubtedly a bird, as
proved by the faint impressions of flight
feathers in the limestone block.

MAMMALS

THE TRUE MAMMALS had an unimpressive beginning
as small, shrewlike animals more than 210 million
years ago. For a time, the true mammals coexisted
with their close relatives, the mammal-like
reptiles. After the extinction of
the dinosaurs at the end
of the Cretaceous
period, the true
mammals became
both varied and
very numerous.

Pubis

*Ball and
socket joining
leg and pelvis*

*Large ribcage
to protect
huge stomach*

TYPICAL LENGTH
2.75 IN (7 CM)

*Stocky leg for
supporting
large weight*

*Jaws with
sharp teeth*

*Five-toed foot to
hold up massive body*

PALAEOCHIROPTERYX
Eocene
This is the entire fossil skeleton of an extinct bat.
The digits (finger bones) are extremely elongated.
A membrane of skin was stretched between the
digits, forming the wings. The shape of the teeth
suggests that *Palaeochiropteryx* hunted insects.

Double-rooted molar teeth with high, sharp-edged cusps for cutting up food

Broken at rear where muscles were attached

Tooth root

Socket for missing tooth

MORGANUCODON
L. Triassic
This is the fossilized lower jaw of one of the first true mammals. Typical mammal characteristics are the single-piece jawbone and the presence of molar teeth.

TYPICAL LENGTH
10 FT (3 M)

Deep-set eye socket

Bony horn with furrows left by blood vessels

Nostril

ARSINOITHERIUM
L. Oligocene
This massive skeleton belongs to an extinct rhinoceros-like mammal. The impressive pair of horns were made of bone, unlike the horns of a rhinoceros, which are made of compressed hair. The animal's teeth show that it fed mainly on leaves.

MAMMAL FACTS
• *Morganucodon* measured less than two inches (a few centimeters) in length, and weighed a mere 0.7 oz (20 gm).
• The oldest known mammal fossils are the teeth of *Haramiya*.

HIPPARION
20 MILLION YEARS AGO

Mammal expansion

The extinction of the dinosaurs left the world open for the mammals. The first mammals to take advantage of the situation were the marsupials (pouched mammals). Today, most marsupials are found in Australasia along with the monotremes (egg-laying mammals). Throughout the rest of the world, placental mammals proved more successful, and they are now the dominant land animals.

HYRACOTHERIUM
50 MILLION YEARS AGO

HORSE DEVELOPMENT
Early horses, such as *Hyracotherium,* lived in forests. Later, they moved onto grassland plains, where they were more visible to predators. Their only defense was increased speed, made possible by longer legs and fewer toes.

Cheek teeth

Nasal opening

TYPICAL LENGTH 5 FT (1.5 M)

THYLACOLEO
Pliocene–Pleistocene
This fossil skull belongs to a lionlike marsupial predator from Australia. The large cheek teeth were very effective blades for cutting through flesh. The lower jaw is missing in this specimen.

Tusks of Stegodon were 10 ft (3 m) long

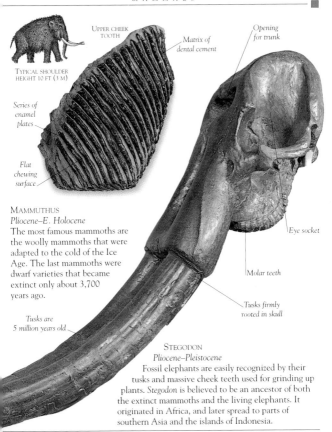

UPPER CHEEK TOOTH

Matrix of dental cement

Opening for trunk

TYPICAL SHOULDER HEIGHT 10 FT (3 M)

Series of enamel plates

Flat chewing surface

Eye socket

Molar teeth

Tusks firmly rooted in skull

MAMMUTHUS
Pliocene–E. Holocene
The most famous mammoths are the woolly mammoths that were adapted to the cold of the Ice Age. The last mammoths were dwarf varieties that became extinct only about 3,700 years ago.

Tusks are 5 million years old

STEGODON
Pliocene–Pleistocene
Fossil elephants are easily recognized by their tusks and massive cheek teeth used for grinding up plants. *Stegodon* is believed to be an ancestor of both the extinct mammoths and the living elephants. It originated in Africa, and later spread to parts of southern Asia and the islands of Indonesia.

Giant mammals

The last 50 million years have seen significant changes in mammals. A number of previously important groups have become extinct, such as the first hoofed mammals (the condylarths) and the first successful carnivores (the creodonts). The ancestry of most living mammals can be traced back to these early placental mammals. Since the Ice Age, other groups have become extinct, including many large plant-eaters.

Molar teeth

Eye socket

TYPICAL LENGTH
10 FT (3 M)

PROCOPTODON
Pleistocene
This incomplete fossil jawbone belongs to one of the largest known kangaroos. This extinct marsupial had long forelimbs. It may have been a grazer that used all four limbs for running. The long forelimbs may have helped it browse on high foliage.

Incisors

Well-worn molar teeth

TOXODON
Pleistocene
This ponderous, hoofed mammal was the size of a rhinoceros. Its teeth show that it was a plant-eater. *Toxodon* was the last of the large hoofed mammals to have lived in South America. They became extinct soon after North and South America became joined.

TYPICAL LENGTH 10 FT (3 M)

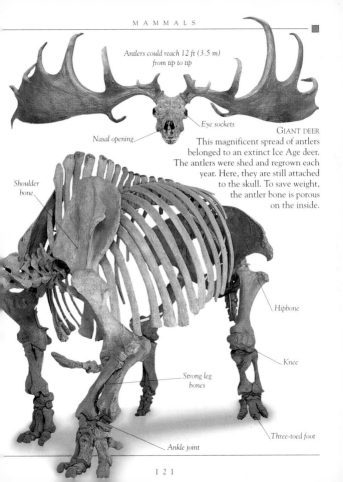

Antlers could reach 12 ft (3.5 m) from tip to tip

Eye sockets

Nasal opening

Shoulder bone

Hipbone

Knee

Strong leg bones

Three-toed foot

Ankle joint

GIANT DEER

This magnificent spread of antlers belonged to an extinct Ice Age deer. The antlers were shed and regrown each year. Here, they are still attached to the skull. To save weight, the antler bone is porous on the inside.

HOMINOIDS AND HOMINIDS

APES AND PEOPLE are grouped together as hominoids because of shared biological features. The fossil record shows that the earliest hominoids originated more than 35 million years ago. Human ancestors belong to a smaller group called hominids. The earliest hominid fossils, such as "Lucy," were found in Africa and are nearly four million years old.

HOMO SAPIENS
The fossil remains of modern humans date back about 100,000 years. Our ancestors lived alongside Neanderthals, and were characterized by domed foreheads, prominent chins, and lighter skeletons.

HOMINOID FACTS
• 99% of chimpanzee DNA is identical to that of humans.
• The oldest known stone tools were made in Africa by *Homo habilis* about 1.9 million years ago.

Neanderthal braincase had about the same capacity as a modern human's

NEANDERTHALS
This is the fossil skull of a powerfully built ice age hunter. Neanderthals were close relatives of living humans. They survived much of the ice age, but died out some 30,000 years ago.

Point where spine joins skull

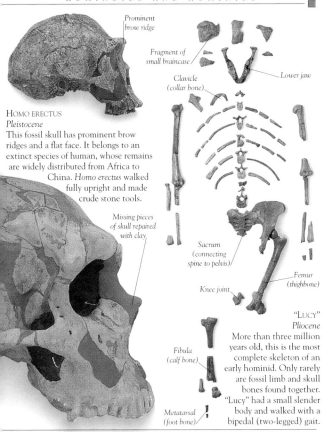

Prominent
brow ridge

Fragment of
small braincase

Clavicle
(collar bone)

Lower jaw

HOMO ERECTUS
Pleistocene
This fossil skull has prominent brow
ridges and a flat face. It belongs to an
extinct species of human, whose remains
are widely distributed from Africa to
China. *Homo erectus* walked
fully upright and made
crude stone tools.

Missing pieces
of skull repaired
with clay

Sacrum
(connecting
spine to pelvis)

Femur
(thighbone)

Knee joint

"LUCY"
Pliocene
More than three million
years old, this is the most
complete skeleton of an
early hominid. Only rarely
are fossil limb and skull
bones found together.
"Lucy" had a small slender
body and walked with a
bipedal (two-legged) gait.

Fibula
(calf bone)

Metatarsal
(foot bone)

PLANTS

PALEOZOIC

SIMPLE MULTICELLED PLANTS, such as algae, have been found as fossils in Precambrian rocks. For a long time, plants, like animals, were confined to water. The development of multicelled land plants during the Silurian period required special structures to stay upright and to prevent them from drying out in the air.

Layered structure

TYPICAL HEIGHT
10 FT (3 M)

COLLENIA
Precambrian–Cambrian
This photograph shows a slice through a fossil algal mound. The layered structure formed by the algae is very similar to living stromatolites. Layers of sediment trapped by the algae have turned into limestone.

Limestone

TYPICAL HEIGHT
10 IN (25 CM)

Mudstone

Stems

Sporangia on
side of stem

Layers of
sediment
bonded together

ZOSTEROPHYLLUM
L. Silurian–M. Devonian
This kind of plant and its relatives are
thought to be among the early ancestors
of club mosses. Each stem carried several
spore-bearing capsules, called sporangia,
along its side. *Zosterophyllum* probably
grew in marshy wetland habitats.

TYPICAL HEIGHT
3 IN (7.5 CM)

Sporangia

"Y" branch

COOKSONIA
L. Silurian–L. Devonian
This tiny fossil is the remains of the oldest
known vascular plant capable of growing on
land. It had a simple "Y"-shaped stem with
oval sporangia at the end. The stem was
strengthened by special cells to keep it upright.

First forests

During the Mississippian and Pennsylvanian periods, much of the land was covered by swampy forests of ferns, club mosses, and horsetails. Today, most of the surviving varieties of these plants are quite small. During the late Paleozoic era, however, they reached the size of modern trees. Some forests were so dense that they formed thick peat deposits that have turned into coal.

ALETHOPTERIS
Pennsylvanian–E. Permian
Fossil impressions of tree-fern fronds are very common in some Pennsylvanian rocks. The ferns grew in the drier parts of tropical swamps. Their accumulated stems form a major part of some coal deposits.

Ironstone nodule

Frond leaflet

TYPICAL HEIGHT
16.5 FT (5 M)

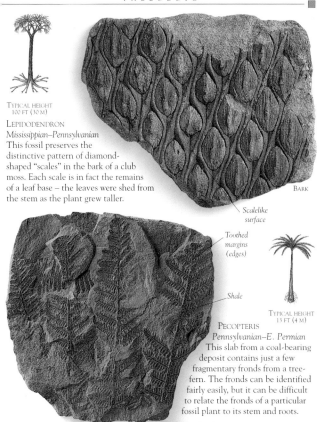

TYPICAL HEIGHT
100 FT (30 M)

LEPIDODENDRON
Mississippian–Pennsylvanian
This fossil preserves the
distinctive pattern of diamond-
shaped "scales" in the bark of a club
moss. Each scale is in fact the remains
of a leaf base – the leaves were shed from
the stem as the plant grew taller.

BARK

Scalelike
surface

Toothed
margins
(edges)

Shale

TYPICAL HEIGHT
13 FT (4 M)

PECOPTERIS
Pennsylvanian–E. Permian
This slab from a coal-bearing
deposit contains just a few
fragmentary fronds from a tree-
fern. The fronds can be identified
fairly easily, but it can be difficult
to relate the fronds of a particular
fossil plant to its stem and roots.

MESOZOIC

THE ANCIENT Paleozoic plants lost their importance
during the Mesozoic era and were overtaken by new
groups. The large club mosses decreased drastically
and conifers became more varied and widespread.
Large ferns declined more slowly while ginkgos and
cycads became abundant. The ability of these plants
to produce seeds enabled
them to colonize
the drier regions.

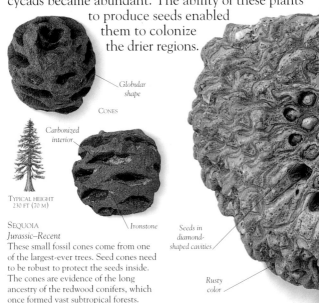

Globular shape

CONES

Carbonized interior

TYPICAL HEIGHT
230 FT (70 M)

SEQUOIA

Jurassic–Recent

Ironstone

These small fossil cones come from one
of the largest-ever trees. Seed cones need
to be robust to protect the seeds inside.
The cones are evidence of the long
ancestry of the redwood conifers, which
once formed vast subtropical forests.

Seeds in diamond-shaped cavities

Rusty color

GINKGO
L. Triassic–Recent
This remarkable survivor is a classic "living fossil." Ginkgos were thought to have become extinct during the Pliocene epoch until some were discovered growing in a Chinese temple garden. Now widespread in ornamental gardens, ginkgos are probably extinct in the wild.

Fan-shaped leaf

TYPICAL HEIGHT
115 FT (35 M)

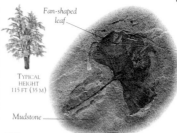

Mudstone

ARAUCARIA
Jurassic–Recent
This fossil cone belongs to a conifer that is commonly known as the monkey-puzzle tree. The small, spiky leaves covered the branches in tight spirals. Once widespread in mountain forests, it is now found in a wild state only in the Southern Hemisphere.

Broken surface

TYPICAL HEIGHT
100 FT (30 M)

PLANT FACTS
• Pollination by insects began during the Jurassic period, but did not become widespread until the Cretaceous period.

• *Araucaria* trees were a common source of fossil amber resin.

Flowering plants

The most important feature of late Mesozoic times was the development of angiosperms (flowering plants). The identification of angiosperm fossils is quite difficult, because many leaves look very similar. The first flowers appeared during the early part of the Cretaceous period, but it was not until the late Cretaceous that flowering plants spread worldwide. Angiosperms now dominate most plant communities on Earth.

Woody outer layer

FRUIT

NIPA
L. Cretaceous–Recent
This coconut-like fossil fruit has a tough, woody outer layer over a fibrous husk that protects the seeds inside. Fossil fruits of angiosperm palms are often found when all other traces of the plant have disappeared.

TYPICAL HEIGHT 5 FT (1.5 M)

Ironstone

Heart-shaped leaf

BETULITES
L. Cretaceous–Miocene
This sandstone mold of a leaf closely resembles a modern birch leaf. Both the leaf shape and the venation (pattern of veins) help identify the plant. Mesozoic birches shed their leaves like modern birches.

TYPICAL HEIGHT 33 FT (10 M)

Leaf margin (edge) is completely smooth

Three-lobed leaf

Central vein

Stalk

Secondary vein comes off at 45°

Sandstone

PLATANOID
L. Cretaceous
The distinctive leaf shape identifies this plant as a member of the ginseng family. The preservation of leaves as fossils depends largely on the habitat in which the plant grew. Lakeside and riverside sediments yield the most plant fossils.

TYPICAL HEIGHT
33 FT (10 M)

CENOZOIC

EARLY CENOZOIC PLANTS grew in extensive forests
and swamps. There was a rich variety of
woody angiosperms, conifers, palms, and
ferns. Many of these plants were very
widely distributed, and the angiosperms
diversified very rapidly. Much of
our knowledge of these plants
comes from studying their pollen.
Microscopic fossil pollen grains
are common in fine-grained
sedimentary rocks.

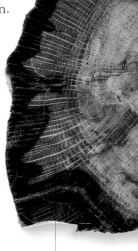

Distinct ray
structure

ACER
Oligocene–Recent
This piece of freshwater limestone contains
the clearly recognizable fruit of the maple.
The plant produces clusters of flowers that,
after pollination, develop into fruit. The
wings enable the seeds to be dispersed easily
by the wind.

WINGED
FRUIT

*Single wing
with veins*

TYPICAL HEIGHT
82 FT (25 M)

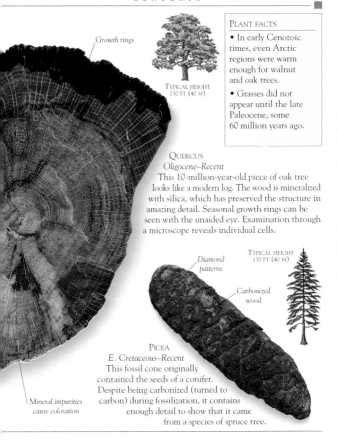

Growth rings

TYPICAL HEIGHT
130 FT (40 M)

PLANT FACTS

• In early Cenozoic times, even Arctic regions were warm enough for walnut and oak trees.

• Grasses did not appear until the late Paleocene, some 60 million years ago.

QUERCUS
Oligocene–Recent
This 10-million-year-old piece of oak tree looks like a modern log. The wood is mineralized with silica, which has preserved the structure in amazing detail. Seasonal growth rings can be seen with the unaided eye. Examination through a microscope reveals individual cells.

TYPICAL HEIGHT
130 FT (40 M)

Diamond patterns

Carbonized wood

PICEA
E. Cretaceous–Recent
This fossil cone originally contained the seeds of a conifer. Despite being carbonized (turned to carbon) during fossilization, it contains enough detail to show that it came from a species of spruce tree.

Mineral impurities cause coloration

135

Today's plants

Late Cenozoic times saw considerable changes in the global flora, resulting in vegetation very similar to that of today. There were fewer kinds of conifer, but more ferns and flowering plants. This last group became increasingly dominant as grasses developed in the Eocene. These formed a new kind of landscape – prairie-type grasslands, which were soon exploited by new groups of grazing mammals.

Husk
(seed cover)

Hairs

Base of
husk

BERRIOCHLOA
L. Miocene
This fossil grass husk is "mummified," preserved by dehydration without decay or flattening. Even though it is some 10 million years old, tiny details can be seen clearly.

BUDDING TWIG
This freshwater limestone preserves the impression of a budding twig. Fine-grained lake and delta deposits often accumulate plant debris from a wide area. Most of the plants are fragments swept down by rivers.

Bud

Fossil flower

PRESERVED PETALS
Fossil flowers, like this Miocene *Porana*, are uncommon. Petals are delicate and required rapid burial in fine-grained sediment to be preserved. The shape and petal structure are very similar to those of living flowers.

TYPICAL HEIGHT
82 FT (25 M)

Five-lobed leaf

Limestone

Black carbonized
film

Simple
venation

LIQUIDAMBAR
Oligocene–Recent
A fossil sweetgum leaf is well
preserved in this specimen from
a freshwater lake deposit. Some of the
original plant is still present in the form of
a patchy film of carbonized material. The leaf
was prevented from decaying in the normal manner
by the lack of oxygen in lake-bottom mud.

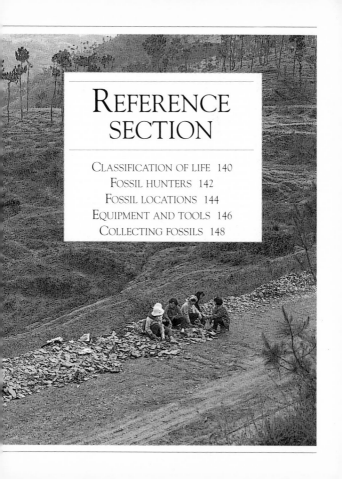

REFERENCE
SECTION

CLASSIFICATION OF LIFE

LIVING THINGS are arranged in groups for scientific convenience. According to present thinking, there are five kingdoms of life that are subdivided into smaller groups. This chart shows the main groups of bacteria, protists, fungi, plants, and animals.

The five kingdoms

Kingdoms in bold capitals – e.g., **MONERA**
Phyla or divisions in small capitals – e.g., EUBACTERIA
Subphyla or subdivisions in bold – e.g., **Vertebrata**
Classes in italics – e.g., *Mammalia*

Extinct groups marked *

MONERA
ARCHAEBACTERIA
("ancient" bacteria)
EUBACTERIA
("true" bacteria and
blue-green algae)

PROTISTA
about 20 phyla including:
HAPTOPHYTA (coccoliths)
RHIZOPODA (foraminiferans)
ACTINOPODA (radiolarians)
BACILLARIOPHYTA (diatoms)
CILIOPHORA (ciliates)

FUNGI
ZYGOMYCOTA
ASCOMYCOTA
DEUTEROMYCOTA
BASIDIOMYCOTA
MYCOPHYCOPHYTA

PLANTAE
RHODOPHYTA (red algae)
PHAEOPHYTA (brown algae)
CHLOROPHYTA (green algae)
BRYOPHYTA (mosses and worts)
LYCOPODIOPHYTA (club mosses)
SPHENOPHYTA (horsetails)
CYCADOPHYTA (cycads)
PTERIDOPHYTA (ferns)
GINKGOPHYTA (ginkgos)
CONIFEROPHYTA (conifers)
GNETOPHYTA (welwitschia)
PSILOPHYTA (whisk ferns)

ANGIOSPERMOPHYTA	
Monocotyledonae	**Dicotyledonae**
e.g.,	e.g.,
Lilicae (lilies)	*Rosaceae* (roses)
Poaceae (wheat)	*Fabaceae* (beans)
Iridaceae (irises)	*Apiaceae* (carrots)
Arecaceae (palms)	*Salicaceae* (willows)
Juncaceae (rushes)	*Solanaceae* (potatoes)
Musaceae (bananas)	*Malvaceae* (hibiscuses)
Cyperaceae (sedges)	*Fagaceae* (oaks)
Gramineae (grasses)	*Cactaceae* (cacti)

ANIMALIA – about 35 phyla including:

PORIFERA (sponges, archaeocyathids*)
PLATYHELMINTHES (flatworms)
NEMATODA (roundworms)
ANNELIDA (segmented worms)
CTENOPHORA (comb jellies)

ROTIFERA (rotifers)
BRYOZOA (bryozoans)
TARDIGRADA (water bears)
BRACHIOPODA (brachiopods)
HEMICHORDATA (graptolites*)

MOLLUSCA
Gastropoda (snails, slugs)
Bivalvia (clams, scallops)
Cephalopoda (squid, ammonites,* belemnites*)

CNIDARIA
Hydrozoa (hydroids)
Scyphozoa (jellyfish)
Anthozoa (corals)

ECHINODERMATA
Crinoidea (sea lilies)
Asteroidea (starfish)
Echinoidea (sea urchins)
*Blastoidea** (blastoids)

ARTHROPODA

Chelicerata
Arachnida (spiders, scorpions)
Merostomata (horseshoe crabs)

Crustacea
Malacostraca (crabs)
Cirripedia (barnacles)

Uniramia
Insecta (insects)
Myriapoda (centipedes, millipedes)

Trilobitidea*
(trilobites)

CHORDATA

Urochordata
(sea squirts)

Cephalochordata
(amphioxous)

Vertebrata:
*Conodonta** (conodont animals)
Agnatha (jawless fish)
*Placodermi** (plated fish)
*Acanthodii** (spiny sharks)
Chondrichthyes (cartilaginous fish)
Osteichthyes (bony fish)
Amphibia (amphibians)
Reptilia (reptiles)
Aves (birds)

Mammalia

subclass Prototheria
Monotremata (egg-laying mammals)

subclass Theria – 18 orders including:
Marsupalia (pouched mammals);
Rodentia (rats and mice); Carnivora (cats and dogs); Cetacea (whales); Creodonta* (primitive meat-eaters); Primates (monkeys)

FOSSIL HUNTERS

FOSSILS WERE KNOWN to the ancient Greeks, but it was not until the eighteenth century that scientists became interested in fossils. During the nineteenth century, the study of fossils made rapid progress. The people on these pages are representative of those who made a contribution to the study of fossils.

MARY ANNING
1799–1847
The most famous member of an English family of professional fossil hunters, Mary found the first complete icthyosaur fossil.

JOACHIM BARRANDE
1799–1883
A French engineer who spent most of his life in Czechoslovakia. He devoted himself to the description of thousands of Paleozoic fossils from Bohemia.

JOHN WOODWARD
1665–1728
An English professor of medicine who collected natural objects including fossils. His collection can still be seen at the University of Cambridge.

GEORGE CUVIER
1769–1832
A French anatomist, he was the greatest naturalist of his day. He showed how a fossil animal can be reconstructed from just a few bones.

ADOLPHE BRONGNIART
1801–76
The son of a French geologist, he was a botanist who pioneered the study of fossil plants, and published a detailed account of his studies.

JEAN LOUIS AGASSIZ
1807–73
A Swiss-born naturalist who spent much of his life in the US. He made important studies of fossil fishes and developed a theory of ice ages.

JAMES HALL
1811-98
A pioneer of the study of fossils in the US. He studied Paleozoic fossils in New York State, where he later became head of the NY Museum of Natural History.

KARL ZITTEL
1830–1904
A German scientist who was professor of geology in Munich. He wrote several handbooks of fossils and a history of the study of fossils.

EDWARD DRINKER COPE
1840–97
A great American naturalist, he spent a fortune collecting fossils. His collection is now in the American Museum of Natural History.

CHARLES WALCOTT
1850–1927
An American geologist who began collecting fossils as a boy. He discovered the Burgess Shale deposits and other Cambrian fossils.

CHARLES DARWIN
1809–82
An English naturalist who studied both fossil and living organisms. His theory of evolution explains how organisms develop over time.

OTHNIEL MARSH
1831–99
An American professor of natural history, he competed with his rival Edward Cope to collect new dinosaur fossils from the American West.

FLORENTINO AMEGHINO
1854–1911
An Argentinian scientist who, together with his brother Carlo, collected and studied many South American fossil dinosaurs and mammals.

FOSSIL LOCATIONS

FOSSILS ARE FOUND on every continent
and in every country. This map shows
some of the many important
fossil sites throughout
the world.

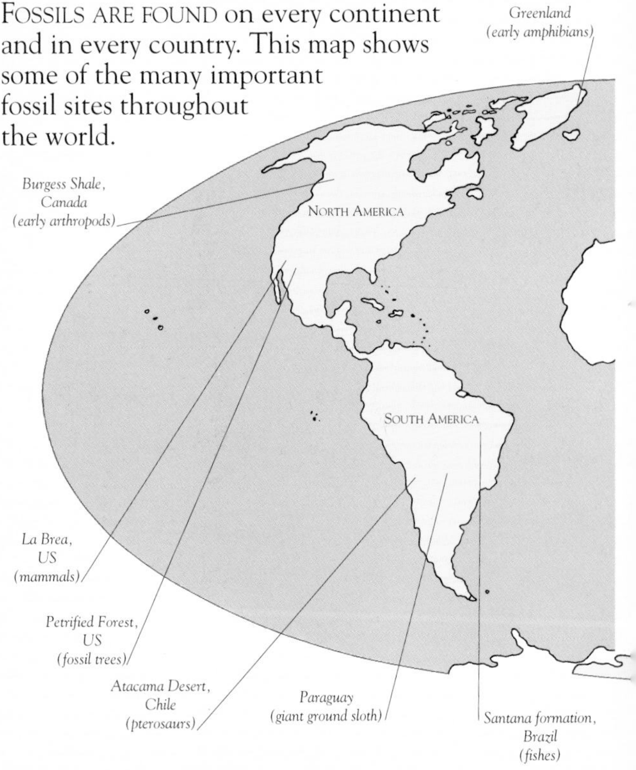

Greenland
(early amphibians)

NORTH AMERICA

Burgess Shale,
Canada
(early arthropods)

SOUTH AMERICA

La Brea,
US
(mammals)

Petrified Forest,
US
(fossil trees)

Atacama Desert,
Chile
(pterosaurs)

Paraguay
(giant ground sloth)

Santana formation,
Brazil
(fishes)

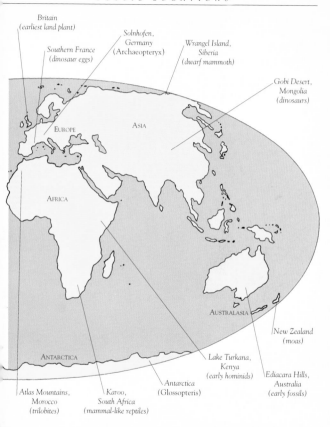

Britain
(earliest land plant)

Solnhofen,
Germany
(Archaeopteryx)

Southern France
(dinosaur eggs)

Wrangel Island,
Siberia
(dwarf mammoth)

Gobi Desert,
Mongolia
(dinosaurs)

EUROPE

ASIA

AFRICA

AUSTRALASIA

New Zealand
(moas)

ANTARCTICA

Atlas Mountains,
Morocco
(trilobites)

Karoo,
South Africa
(mammal-like reptiles)

Antarctica
(Glossopteris)

Lake Turkana,
Kenya
(early hominids)

Ediacara Hills,
Australia
(early fossils)

EQUIPMENT AND TOOLS

COLLECTING FOSSILS is a safe and enjoyable pastime if you use the right equipment. The opposite is also true; trying to collect fossils without the proper equipment can be frustrating and hazardous. The tools and equipment shown here will enable you to extract safely most of the fossils that you find.

GLOVES

HARD HAT

GOGGLES

Guard protects hand

Geologist's hammer has point for splitting rock

GUARDED CHISELS

GEOLOGIST'S HAMMER

MALLET

TROWEL

WHAT TO WEAR

A hard hat is essential for protecting your head from falling rocks. Goggles protect your eyes from dust and rock fragments. Gloves protect your hands from sharp rocks.

FOSSIL TOOLS

A geologist's hammer is the single most useful tool for removing small fossils. Larger specimens may need a separate hammer and chisels. A builder's trowel is very useful for searching through dirt, mud, and other soft deposits.

CLEANING AND PREPARATION

Old paintbrushes and toothbrushes can be used to remove mud and soil. Dental tools can also be used to pick and scrape pieces of hard matrix from the fossil. Always be sure to wear safety goggles to protect your eyes when "picking" at a fossil.

TOOTHBRUSH

SMALL PAINTBRUSH

TWEEZERS

PAINTBRUSHES   DENTAL TOOLS

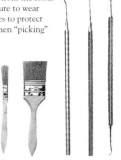

TAKING NOTES

Make a note of the location of every fossil that you find. If necessary, draw a sketch showing the location. A wirebound notebook is most useful. Pages can be torn out and used to wrap small fossils, without spoiling your record keeping.

PENS AND NOTEBOOK

Lens folds into handle for carrying

MAGNIFYING GLASS

SEEING SMALL DETAILS

A magnifying glass often comes in handy for examining your fossils more closely. If possible, choose a folding model that can be carried easily in your pocket without damaging the lens.

COLLECTING FOSSILS

FOSSIL COLLECTING can be great fun. Any fossil that
you find has probably never been seen by another
human, and it may even be new to science.
So take care of your fossil, and clean it
carefully. Try looking it up in a book
and, if you think it may be unusual,
take it to your local museum.

*Beware of
falling rocks*

*Do not collect on
unstable slopes of
loose material*

SENSIBLE COLLECTING
• Make sure that you are allowed to
collect fossils from a site.
• Make sure it is safe to collect – stay
away from cliffs and overhangs.
• Wear suitable clothing and safety
gear, and have the right equipment.
• Tell someone where you are going
and what time you expect to return.

*Collect safely
at the bottom
of a slope*

• Don't be greedy and
take all the fossils from
a site. Leave some for
other collectors.

AT HOME

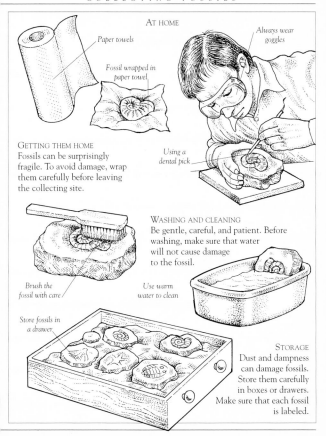

Paper towels

Fossil wrapped in paper towel

Always wear goggles

Using a dental pick

GETTING THEM HOME
Fossils can be surprisingly fragile. To avoid damage, wrap them carefully before leaving the collecting site.

Brush the fossil with care

WASHING AND CLEANING
Be gentle, careful, and patient. Before washing, make sure that water will not cause damage to the fossil.

Use warm water to clean

Store fossils in a drawer

STORAGE
Dust and dampness can damage fossils. Store them carefully in boxes or drawers. Make sure that each fossil is labeled.

Resources

US

Academy of Natural Sciences of Philadelphia
1900 Benjamin Franklin Parkway
Philadelphia, PA 19103

American Museum of Natural History
Central Park West at 79th Street
New York, NY 10024

Buffalo Museum of Science
1020 Humboldt Parkway
Buffalo, NY 14211

Carnegie Museum of Natural History
4400 Forbes Avenue
Pittsburgh, PA 15213

Cleveland Museum of Natural History
Wade Oval Drive
University Circle
Cleveland, OH 44106

Denver Museum of Natural History
2001 Colorado Boulevard
Denver, CO 80205

Dinosaur National Monument
P.O. Box 128
Jensen, UT 84035

Earth Science Museum
Brigham Young University
1683 North Canyon Road
Provo, UT 84602

Exhibit Museum
University of Michigan
1109 Geddes Avenue
Ann Arbor, MI 48109

Field Museum of Natural History
Roosevelt Road at Lake Shore Drive
Chicago, IL 60605

Fort Worth Museum of Science and Technology
1501 Montgomery Street
Fort Worth, TX 76107

Geological Museum
University of Wyoming
Box 3254
Laramie, WY 82071

Houston Museum of Natural Science
1 Hermann Circle Drive
Houston, TX 77030

Museum of Comparative Zoology
26 Oxford Street
Harvard University
Cambridge, MA 02138

Museum of Northern Arizona
Rt. 4 Box 720
Flagstaff, AZ 86001

Museum of Paleontology
University of California
197 McCone Hall
Berkeley, CA 94720

Museum of Science and History
1025 Museum Circle
Jacksonville, FL 32207

Museum of the Rockies
Montana State University
Bozeman, MT 59717

National Museum of Natural History
Smithsonian Institution
Washington, DC 20560

**Natural History
Museum of
Los Angeles County**
900 Exposition Boulevard
Los Angeles, CA 90007

**North Carolina State
Museum of
Natural Sciences**
102 North Southbury
Street
Raleigh, NC 27603

**Peabody Museum of
Natural History**
Yale University
170 Whitney Avenue
New Haven, CT 06511

**Pratt Museum of
Natural History**
Amherst College
Amherst, MA 01002

Red Mountain Museum
1421 22nd Street South
Birmingham, AL 35205

**Utah Museum of
Natural History**
University of Utah
1350 East, 200 South
Salt Lake City, UT 84112

CANADA
**Calgary Zoo,
Botanical Garden
and Prehistoric Park**
P.O. Box 3036,
Station B
Calgary, ALB T2M 4R8

**Canadian Museum
of Nature**
National Museum
of Canada
240 McLeod Avenue
Ottawa, ONT K1A 0M8

Dinosaur Provincial Park
P.O. Box 60,
Patricia, ALB P0J 2K0

Geological Museum
University of
Saskatchewan
Department of Geological
Sciences
Saskatoon, SK S7N 0W0

**Geological Survey
of Canada**
601 Booth Street
Ottawa, ONT K1A 0E8

**Manitoba Museum of
Man and Nature**
190 Rupert Avenue
Winnipeg, MAN R3B 0N2

**Nova Scotia Museum
of Natural History**
1747 Summer Street
Halifax, NS B3H 3A6

**Provincial Museum
of Alberta**
12845 102nd Avenue
Edmonton, ALB T5N 0M6

Redpath Museum
McGill University
859 Sherbrook Street West
Montreal, QUE H3A 2K6

Royal Ontario Museum
100 Queen's Park
Toronto, ONT M5S 2C6

**Saskatchewan Museum
of Natural History**
Wascana Park
Regina, SK S4P 3Z7

**Tyrrell Museum
of Paleontology**
Highway 838
Midland Provincial Park
Drumheller, ALB T0J 0Y0

Glossary

AGNATHAN
Jawless – usually refers to the jawless fish that are common fossils in Devonian rocks.

ALGAE
A major group of simple aquatic plants that includes seaweed.

AMBER
Fossilized tree resin.

AMMONITE
Extinct group of marine cephalopods that lived in coiled shells.

AMPHIBIAN
One of a major grouping of vertebrates – those that are tetrapod when adult but must return to water to breed.

ANAPSIDS
One of the subgroups into which reptiles are classified.

ANGIOSPERMS
A major group of plants – the flowering plants.

APPENDAGE
A mobile extension of an animal's body.

ARTHROPOD
A member of the group of invertebrates, having an exoskeleton and jointed legs.

ASPHALT
The tarry residue left when all the gases have evaporated from natural oil deposits.

BELEMNITE
One of an extinct group of marine mollusks that resembled modern squid.

BIOLOGY
The scientific study of living organisms.

BRACHIOPODS
A group of mollusklike marine animals.

BRACT
A modified flower-bearing leaf.

BRYOZOANS
A major group of colonial marine invertebrates. Also called "moss animals."

BYSSUS
Tough, organic thread used by some bivalves to anchor themselves.

CALCAREOUS
Made of a mineral of calcium, usually in the form of a carbonate.

CALICE
The upper surface of the cup in which a coral polyp lives.

CARAPACE
The mineralized skeleton of certain arthropods, e.g., crabs.

CARBONIZATION
The process by which a residue of carbon replaces the original material of an organic substance.

CARTILAGINOUS
Having an internal skeleton made of non-mineralized material.

CENOZOIC
The most recent era of geologic time.

CEPHALOPOD
One of a large group of marine mollusks, e.g., squid and the extinct ammonites and belemnites.

CLASS
A grouping of related orders of organisms, e.g., birds (Class Aves).

COLONY
A group of genetically related individuals that may also be linked together to form an organism.

CONODONTS
Small fossil teeth which are now thought to have belonged to a group of early vertebrates.

CORALLITE
The calcareous skeleton secreted by one of the polyps in a coral colony.

CRINOID
A sea lily, a plantlike animal related to starfish and sea urchins.

CRUSTACEAN
One of a group of marine arthropods that includes crabs.

DEHYDRATION
The removal of water.

DIAPSIDS
One of the major subdivisions into which reptiles are classified.

DINOSAUR
One of an extinct group of diapsid reptiles.

DNA
Deoxyribonucleic acid, the material that carries the genetic code of organisms.

ECHINOID
A sea urchin.

EPOCH
A division of geologic time within a period.

ERA
A major division of geologic time, subdivided into periods.

EXOSKELETON
The organic covering that protects and supports arthropods.

FAMILY
A grouping of related genera.

FILTER-FEEDING
Describes animals that sieve small food particles from water.

FLINT
A hard, fine-grained, silica rock.

FOSSIL
Preserved evidence of past life.

FOSSILIFEROUS
Containing fossils.

FOSSILIZATION
The processes by which plant or animal remains become preserved.

GASTROPOD
One of a group of mollusks that includes slugs and snails.

GENUS
A grouping of related species. The plural is genera.

GEOLOGY
The scientific study of the Earth and its history.

GRAPTOLITE
An extinct marine, colonial organism.

HOMINIDS
The group that consists of humans and their ancestors.

HOMINOIDS
The group that includes hominids and apes.

HYDROPLANE
A winglike structure for adjusting the angle of a dive.

ICHTHYOSAUR
An extinct marine reptile shaped like a dolphin.

IMPERVIOUS
Describes any material that does not allow fluid to pass through it.

INCISOR
One of the cutting teeth at the front of the mouth.

INDEX FOSSIL
A characteristic fossil species used for dividing rock strata into zones.

INVERTEBRATE
An animal lacking a backbone.

IRON PYRITE
A shiny, gold-colored mineral.

KINGDOM
The largest grouping of organisms, e.g., Kingdom Animalia.

LIGAMENT
Fibrous animal tissue that fastens body parts together.

LIVING FOSSIL
A living organism with characteristics that have remained unchanged over many millions of years.

LOBE
A broad, rounded projection.

LOPHOPHORE
The feeding tentacles around the mouth of some marine animals.

MAMMALS
A major group of animals – those with hair that feed their young on milk.

MAMMOTH
One of an extinct group of elephants, some of which were adapted to cold climates.

MARINE
Living in, or associated with, the sea.

MATRIX
The material in which something (e.g., a fossil) is embedded.

MEMBRANE
A thin, flexible, organic covering.

MESOZOIC
The middle era of fossiliferous geologic time.

MINERALIZATION
The process by which minerals become incorporated into an organic substance.

MOLAR
One of the chewing teeth at the sides of the jaw.

MOLLUSKS
A large group (phylum) of invertebrates with soft bodies, most of which are protected by shells.

MOLT
Shedding of the outer layer of an animal's body to allow for growth.

MONOTREME
An egg-laying mammal.

NODULE
A small, rounded lump.

ORDER
A group of families within a class.

ORGANIC
Anything derived from living organisms, usually containing carbon.

OSSICLE
A small part of a skeleton, especially the calcareous plates of starfish and sea urchins.

PALEOZOIC
The earliest major division of fossiliferous geologic time.

PECTORAL FINS
The foremost fins on a fish's side.

PEDICLE
The fleshy stalk by which some brachiopods anchor themselves.

PELVIC
Relating to the hips.

PERIOD
In geologic time, the subdivision of an era.

PERMAFROST
The permanently frozen ground in polar regions.

PHRAGMOCONE
The chambered part of a cephalopod shell.

PHYLUM
A major grouping of organisms with shared characteristics.

PLACENTAL
Refers to most of the living mammals, whose young develop in the womb, nourished by the placenta.

PLANKTONIC
Describes organisms that float and drift in water.

POLYP
An individual in a coral colony.

POROUS
Describes a substance that allows fluid to pass through it.

PREDATOR
An animal that hunts other animals for food.

REPTILES
A major grouping of animals – those covered with dry, scaly skin.

SEDIMENT
Any material that is deposited in layers on the Earth's surface.

SEPTUM
A wall-like structure in a skeleton.

SILICA
A nonmetallic mineral.

SIPHUNCLE
The tube that extends through the shell of a cephalopod.

SPECIES
The most basic biological grouping of organisms. Members of the same species can interbreed to produce fertile young.

SPICULES
Spine-shaped deposits of minerals that provide some animals with a skeleton-like structure.

STRATA
Layers of sedimentary rock deposited on top of one another, with the oldest rocks at the bottom.

STRATIGRAPHY
The scientific study of rock strata.

STROMATOLITE
A mound-shaped structure made up of layers of calcareous mud held together by filaments of algae.

SYNAPSIDS
One of the extinct subdivisions into which reptiles are classified. Synapsids are also known as the mammal-like reptiles.

TERRESTRIAL
Living on land, or associated with land.

TETRAPOD
An animal with four legs.

THECAE
Cup-shaped part of a skeleton, especially in some colonial marine animals, e.g., graptolites.

TRACE FOSSIL
Markings produced by organisms in the past and preserved in rock.

TRILOBITE
One of a group of extinct marine arthropods.

TUBERCLE
A small, rounded protuberance or knob.

VASCULAR
Refers to those plants that have small tubes within their tissues to transport water and keep them upright.

VERTEBRA
A bone forming part of the backbone.

VERTEBRATE
An animal with a backbone.

ZOOIDS
Closely related, and often interconnected, individuals in a colonial organism.

Index

Acknowledgments

Dorling Kindersley would like to thank: Hilary Bird for the index; Robin Hunter for artwork and design assistance; Kristin Ward for editorial assistance; and William L. Crepet.

Illustrators: Rick Blakely; Peter Bull; Stephen Bull; Lynn Chadwick; Simone End; Will Giles; Andrew Green; Richard Lewis; Andrew MacDonald; Sandra Pond; Mike Saunders; Gill Tomblin; Richard Ward; John Woodcock.

Picture Credits: t = top b = bottom
c = center l = left r = right

Photography: The Natural History Museum, London, except the following: Prof. Larry Agenbroad: 15t; American Museum of Natural History/Lynton Gardiner: 30-31; Dr. D. Bates: 14t; Dr. M. Bell: 14c, 14b; Prof. D.E.G. Briggs: 36b, 69t, 69b; Dr. N. Butterfield: 36t; The Hunterian Museum, Glasgow: 2b, 89c, 90b, 92t; Bruce Coleman/Jules Cowan: 20, Jan Taylor: 45t, Wild-Type Productions: 24t; Mary Evans Picture Library: 142bl, 143br; Dr.

A. Friday: 41tr; Hulton Deutsch: 142t, 143tl, 143tr, 143bl; Dr. E. Jarzembowski: 13br, 35t, 35c; Dr. A. Lister: 29c, 29b; Dr. D. Loydell: 84-85c; Dr. J. Martin: 45c; Natural History Photographic Agency: 41c; Naturmuseum Senckenburg, Frankfurt: 108b, 111b; Dr. C. Peat: 44b; D. Palmer: 15b, 28, 31b, 84b, 142br; Dr. M. Purnell: 88t, 88c, 88b, 89t, 89b, 92t; R.B. Rickards: 84l; Royal Scottish Museum: 34, 91cl; Dr. D. Siveter: 29t, 68t, 68b, 138-139; Sternberg Museum of Natural History, Fort Hays State/Dr. Joseph Thomasson: 136l; Tyrrell Museum of Paleontology: 104-105t, 107b; Yorkshire Museum: 101b, 103c; Additional photography: Colin Keates, Natural History Museum photographer, and Harry Taylor.

Every effort has been made to trace the copyright holders and we apologize in advance for any unintentional omissions. We would be pleased to insert the appropriate acknowledgment in any subsequent edition of this publication.